The First Few Friends I Had

The First Few Friends I Had

love stories from the gone world

Christopher Newton

Pondering Pig Press

Cover design by Mark Lamirande

Published by
Pondering Pig Press
Spokane, Washington

ISBN-13: 978-0-989-710817
First Edition

To my forever Patrushka,

who came later

*While riding on a train goin' west
I fell asleep for to take my rest
I dreamed a dream that made me sad
Concerning myself and the first few friends I
had.*

Bob Dylan

CONTENTS

Peace, Ghosts

On Dead Man's Curve

Baby Beats

Into The Hard Day

The Ghosts in the Corner

Peace, Ghosts

I could blame it on growing old, but I know it's not, not really. I've seen them all my life, these ghosts. They watch me like children who've been sent to the corner.

Some places are more ghostly than others, though, like the corner of Seventh and Judah in San Francisco's Sunset District. I cannot walk past that corner without seeing Solveig coming out the door carrying "Ban The Bomb" placards for the demonstration. She might as well wave at me, but she never does. Or seeing Peter Weissinger swing over the rail of our entry stairs onto teenagers crashing our big peacenik party, and whomp on them in peacenik joy. Or seeing Carmen O'Shaughnessy emerge from that same archway with her long braids, her confident smile, and my Mexican chaleco.

Who are these ghosts, man? Were they ever real? Is this all a dream?

On Dead Man's Curve

San Mateo, California

1958-59

PROLOGUE
This World Can Go Jump

It's the winter of 1958 and here I am in the bathroom of my parents' house on Edna Way, San Mateo, California, locking my D.A. into place with a palm full of Wildroot Cream Oil.

Now I'm slouching down the sidewalk of the ultra-modern subdivision where we live, headed for the school bus stop – dragging my ass past other houses that look just like our house, each with a scrawny flowering plum off-center in its patch of lawn.

Now here I am sitting on a bench in the sun, San Mateo High School, eating my baloney sandwich, pint of milk, two Sno Balls, one pink, one white, trading stupid jokes with Les and Archie, then fifth period doing chemistry homework in study hall but not understanding it or caring.

Now here I am home again after school watching "Topper" reruns, making a salami sandwich with sliced tomatoes and onions, playing poker with the Tanaka brothers across the street.

Now here I am at the basketball game wearing white tonight in the bleachers. Reggie the pep squad leader who someone told me is a homo is doing back flips during intermission. What was a homo anyway? I didn't know and I didn't care. Was this all? There must be more.

I felt like once I had lived in a place that was real when I went out the front door. There were trees in it and cats and a blue sky, but now somehow I'd been washed up in this vacant lot, this blankness. I wanted to go home. See? That's how I felt.

But I *was* home.

Now I'm eating dinner at the built-in Formica breakfast table with Mom and Dad, but not with my brother. He's already been thrown out of his decrepit Chevy coupe on North Delaware Street in a smashup on his way to work at seven o'clock in the morning and fractured his skull on the pavement and now is dead, gone forever in the emergency room at Mills Memorial Hospital at nine o'clock in the morning.

Where was I? There must be another world someplace. There *had* to be or I was sunk. I couldn't explain it, but I was suffocating.

I lay in bed trying not to think of my brother but imagining how someday I'd ride across France on my Lambretta with an existential French girl like Leslie Caron on the back and the sparkling ocean beside us. We would share a loaf of French bread and a bottle of sparkling wine on the sparkling French beach, then look into each other's eyes and make golden love beside the green ocean.

Thank God for sex. I could lie in bed for hours constructing fantasies about how I would get Cindy across the street to take off her clothes and then, if I kept my mind focused on what was under her clothes, I didn't have to feel anything except my hard-on. Maybe she'd let me rub baby oil on her back again while she sunbathed. Maybe she'd let me untie her top when she turned onto her stomach.

Cindy was already out of high school, going to secretarial college. I idolized her, and she accepted my pimply faced presence with grace.

Once, after my brother got creamed, Cindy took me for a long drive out the Skyline Boulevard to La Honda in her baby blue '51 Ford convertible. Its rag-top was buttoned down, the radio on loud to Top 40, and it was the only time I was comforted. I wanted to drive on with Cindy forever to Santa Cruz and Monterey and Big Sur and beyond to Mexico or anywhere else and never go back to death-covered San Mateo.

The Top 40 DJ played "It was a one-eyed, one-horned, flyin' purple people eater" as Cindy steered through the redwood forest and over the verdant April hills.

Cindy must have known how I felt. I never cried about my brother because if I started I would never stop until I died too. She just didn't know how I schemed to get her clothes off. Or maybe she even knew that.

I wished I could still pray. When I was nine my parents sent me to Catholic school although they weren't Catholics. They thought public school was getting too rough for a kid with a heart murmur like me. I liked going to Mass with the other kids, lined up to walk to church next door in our white shirts and tweeduroy pants and our blue button-up sweaters.

I liked it when the priest in his white surplice came down the aisle swinging his incense censer. It made the church smell like holiness and I liked that. I liked it when Sister Mary Angela told us stories about the saints, and how God spoke to them man to man or man to woman.

I liked God and I liked Mary. Jesus was a shining presence in my life. That was in bright San Francisco where the incense mingled with ocean fog and seagulls screeched over our lunch yard. Then we moved to San Mateo where Ozzie and Harriet lived.

Dad was a tough newspaper guy, not religious. Mom was a solitary believer. She meditated. She read books about how God is Love so there can be no evil in the world, just wonderful Love. I looked through her books, and I saw gushing, cloying delirium.

What I wanted in my deepest heart was not gushing pretend love. I wanted war.

I began to question if anything the sisters had taught me was true. Turning water into wine? How do you do that? Water is hydrogen and oxygen. Coming back to life after you're dead? I wish! Life! Stupid fucking life. Here it comes...stupid fucking world killed my brother! Nothing is true. It's all a fraud, all fake. Fake Fake FAKE! If my brother can get killed in a car crash then the whole world can go jump. Fuck off!

Somewhere that year I declared war on the world as I knew it then, the whole vast unreal wasteland of it. I wanted nothing more to do with their religion and their politics and their backyard barbecues and their anticommunist crusades and their race to space and their fucking success mentality and get a good job and live in a mansion and own a Rolls-Royce. I'm walking!

This was the state of my 16-year-old heart as I jumped up and down in the bleachers at the basketball game and tugged Betty Hammond's ponytail and plotted how I would one day get Cindy to take off her clothes. I buried my rage behind a laugh and a happy-go-lucky smile. But I was a torch waiting for a match and the match was *The Dharma Bums.* Thank you Jack Kerouac forever and flowers on your grave.

The Baby Dharma Bums

Now it's a few days before Christmas 1958 and I am standing in the crowded aisle of the Hillsdale Bookshop, reading *The Dharma Bums*. Shoppers are pushing around me to grab a copy of the best seller everybody wants to put on their coffee table but nobody wants to read, *Dr. Zhivago*. Somewhere nearby, Alvin the Chipmunk is bitching to Santa, something about a hula hoop.

I'd driven to the Hillsdale Mall after school to buy my mother a Christmas present, but instead I found myself riding a boxcar up the California coast, meditating on the actual warmth of God. Next I hitched a long zipping ride all the way to Grant Avenue in North Beach with a way-out blonde high on bennies in her baby blue '51 Ford convertible. My Beat Generation friends were already there having a great time guzzling wine and smoking pot and shouting crazy poems across the Co-Existence Bagel Shop. I ignored the shoppers bashing their way past me. I had discovered a better way to live.

Although *The Dharma Bums* purported to be a novel, I could tell it was written by a guy who had actually done all these things and was just writing down what happened. I decided in an instant that I was going to do those things too. I had found my calling. I was 16. I had joined the Beat Generation.

You can bet my mother was pleased with an interesting Christmas present like *The Dharma Bums*. I wasn't sure if she would be, but, after all, she *was* interested in spiritual subjects, and *The Dharma Bums* had Buddhism in it.

Besides, it was an expensive hardcover book and I needed to read it 38 more times right away, so it had to be in the house.

I spent the spring working my way through the Kerouac canon: *On The Road, The Subterraneans* (when Mardou Fox walked out on Jack at the end I slammed the paperback against the wall in anger that life should be so bitter, that the one you loved would always leave you in the end), then *Howl*, the best poem I ever read – it had angelheaded hipsters in it – then Gregory Corso's *Gasoline* with its incendiary red and white cover in the Pocket Poets series, then Ferlinghetti's *A Coney Island of the Mind* – so great because I could actually understand it.

Then *Beatitude* magazine, then the *Abomunist Manifesto* – by then I was hip, man. I was beat.

And you know the beauty part? All this was happening just 20 miles away, in my hometown: golden San Francisco. Up there I'd find a world of adventure and pot parties and beatnik chicks in black leotards and poetry and jazz sessions in the cellars of North Beach.

Did that beat San Mateo High School? Or would I rather go to the sock hop with Les and Archie again and ask Betty Hammond to dance the bop while Annette Funicello sang "Tall Paul is my love, tall Paul is my dream, he's the captain of the high school football team"?

Let me think...I know! I would rather, much rather, incredibly rather, be beat.

One day I was sitting in geometry reading *A Coney Island of the Mind* when I noticed the tall skinny guy a couple of rows over had curly hairs on his chin. Could he be growing a goatee?

I thought I was the only beat at San Mateo High School!

The cool guy's name was Russ Garibaldi. I started talking to him after class and discovered that he knew all about Jack Kerouac and Allen Ginsberg and that his older sister went to North Beach on weekends and owned sides by big West Coast jazz artists like Bud Shank and Jimmy Giuffre and the Chico Hamilton Quintet. He invited me over to his house after school to listen to her record collection. He introduced me to his beat actor friend Ricky Lazaro. Then Ricky introduced me to his beat artist friend, Way Out Will Staunton. Pretty soon we were all hanging out together.

When Russ and his sister were kids, Russ Garibaldi Senior built a playhouse for them in their backyard and electrified it. It was still in pretty good condition out there in the cabbages and zucchini. We dragged in a mattress and a rickety couch and an existential coffee table of ersatz wood and turned the playhouse into The Pad. My mother donated a madras bedspread for the mattress and lent us one of her paintings, a Zen haiku brush thing featuring green and yellow drips. It was very Dharma Bums, and we loved it.

I scrounged a plastic FM radio so we could listen to KJAZ all night. Best of all, Russ scored an elderly Royal typewriter. I could ease myself over their backyard gate at any hour of the night and be pretty sure a light would be on in The Pad – Russ still up thinking cool and crazy thoughts to the sound of Gerry Mulligan.

We wrote beat poems together, I smoked my pipe (why did I think beats smoked pipes?) and when we got hungry we headed into the Garibaldi kitchen for 2 a.m. feasts of French bread, salami, coffee and, very occasionally, water glasses of homemade wine from the Garibaldi cousins in Stockton.

I still have one of those poems I wrote in The Pad. It's called "Find This in a Typewriter." The imprint of the Royal's ancient half-filled-in letters is unmistakable. I must have written it for Russ to find later but then, for some lost reason, folded it up and slipped it into my notebook instead.

I found it again 40 years later when I closed out my parents' house in San Mateo after Dad died. It wasn't in a typewriter; the notebook had fallen behind a dresser in my old bedroom. In the dust bunnies and mouse droppings, I found it again...

well russ,
this is my battlefield.
here, on this table, at this machine,
my guts will spill, or solidify.
This is where it all ends up, russ,
This is where I justify,
or atrophy.
The word is its own meaning.
But...
What ballroom is this
where the lone dancer drags through dust?
What Victrola scratches on?
Who drew the shades?
Why does that kid sit on the side,
reading about model railroads?
To hell with model railroads!
Sweep the floor!
Break that fucking Virginia Reel!
Get some air in here...
Then bring in the girls!
Let's get started!
sore foot, hell.

On Dead Man's Curve

One night in June 1959, Eddie Tanaka asked me if I wanted to go to a beach party after graduation practice. We were both seniors at San Mateo High, an ivy-covered bastion of conservatism that looked as if Mickey Rooney and Judy Garland should be putting on a show in the gym. Eddie and I had a lot in common. He wasn't a beat poet like me, but he was from the Richmond District, the same San Francisco neighborhood where I'd lived out my childhood. We both despised San Mateo and longed for the foggy streets of the big town.

I invited Tracy from biology, Eddie asked Marilee Blume from his civics class. After rehearsal we took off our gowns, jumped into Eddie's parents' brand-new 1959 Chevy Impala, and raced over the mountains to the Coastside.

A quick geography lesson: The San Francisco Peninsula is divided into three thin strips. The airport and suburbs that bang into one another from San Francisco to San Jose stretch along the Bay on the east side. West of the suburbs lies a wooded ridge, known locally as the Skyline from the highway that traverses it. It's wild country up there even today because the Water Department fenced off its hills long ago. A traveler from San Mateo has to drive right over that ridge and down the other side to get to the third strip, called the Coastside, with its mist-covered hills, beaches below the cliffs, and, in those days, artichoke fields covering the bluffs above the ocean.

In sunny weather, the beaches were about a 45-minute drive from San Mateo, but the road was often enveloped in thick fog. Years later, when I heard Jan and Dean sing, "You

9

won't come back from Dead Man's Curve," I always thought of that road. Kids barreled over it to the Coastside and back every weekend night, passing on curves, then waiting impatiently through long traffic pileups because of a wreck ahead. Eventually an ambulance would shriek by in the oncoming lane and pretty soon traffic would slowly begin moving again.

The beach party was kind of a bust. We found a dozen or so kids huddled around a fire in the chill night. Andy Goodwin had brought his Japanese guitar (in 1959 Japanese still meant "crummy") and was demonstrating his mastery of "Hang down your head, Tom Dooley." We helped finish their case of Olympia half-quarts, then I borrowed Andy's guitar and ripped through my version of "Jailhouse Rock." We hung around for half an hour, the girls were cold, we headed back over the mountain to find something more interesting to do.

Fog drifted across the winding road back over the Skyline. Eddie must have been feeling pretty good behind the wheel of his Daddy's new monster machine, with that 18-year-old dark-haired beauty beside him. He might even try to impress her with his skillful driving. I didn't know what Eddie was thinking; my thoughts were pretty much focused on Tracy's bosom.

We crossed the ridge okay, but coming down the east side toward Crystal Springs Reservoir, Eddie hit gravel on the shoulder of a hairpin turn, lost control, and Eddie and me and Tracy and Marilee Blume and the big green Impala spun out over the cliff and tumbled end over end over end, ka-lump ka-lump ka-lump, down the steep slope toward the heaped rockslide debris at the bottom. Impalas didn't come with seat belts.

Fortunately, I couldn't see the boulders. I was too busy not getting killed. I WILL NOT DIE! Just try it, Death! Not this time! I gritted my teeth and tumbled from floor to roof, out of the back seat into the front seat and over the front seat into the back seat again and into Tracy's petticoats and I bounced against the rear window and we landed upside down at the bottom of the hill.

The first thing I saw as I opened my eyes was Tracy's bottom, decently covered in wholesome white panties and framed by her petticoats. She had landed on her hands and knees in front of me and her skirt had flipped up over her waist during the fall.

Ordinarily, I would have been struck by such an unexpected sight. And I guess I WAS struck by it since I can still see her clearly in my mind's eye, petticoats and all. But, for once, I was more interested in getting the hell out of that Impala before it caught fire or exploded or something.

Tracy and I slithered out the now glassless rear window, then helped Eddie and Marilee snake out from under the front seat. The four of us crawled up the hill, not quite a cliff but close to it, helping ourselves up by grabbing the clumps of coyote bush that dotted it.

Above us, cars had pulled off the road to find out what happened. We could see their headlights glaring into the fog. We scrambled the last 50 feet to the top. Some kids we didn't know waited to give us a hand and wrap us in beach blankets.

The Highway Patrol finally showed up and radioed for an ambulance. We were rushed to the emergency hospital in Redwood City. I didn't realize until they took X-rays that I had climbed the cliff with two crushed vertebrae in my spine. I wasn't thinking about my back in the ambulance. I was thinking how I was going to tell my mother that I had been nearly killed in a car wreck. My brother had been snuffed out only a year before. The same way – in a smashup.

"Mom, I'm OK! Really! I'm just in the Emergency Hospital. Eddie had a little accident. But we're OK! There's nothing to worry about!" I think there might have still been some auburn in her hair that night, but it was gone by morning.

Now I need to skip ahead a year and a half to the winter of 1960.

This time my beat poet pal Russ Garibaldi was driving *his* parents' overpowered 1960 DeSoto. We were heading back to San Mateo after some Saturday night non-event, and the rain was pelting down. Ricky Lazaro rode shotgun, and I was in sitting in the back again, this time with our pal Bear Ragsdale. Russ roared down Black Mountain Road through the rainy winter night when – bam, he missed the curve too.

Sometimes I wonder why any male under the age of, say, 50, is issued a driver's license. We're terrible drivers! We get drunk and drive too fast. We stay sober and drive too fast. We take stupid risks that prove nothing to no one. Just give us bows and arrows and tell us to bring back a mountain lion.

So Russ hit the brakes, but the DeSoto fishtailed out of control across the rain-slick pavement until it suddenly encountered a telephone pole on the left side of the road. Lazaro smashed his forehead into the windshield, I broke my nose against the seat in front of me, and blood began dripping out of both of us onto the dashboard, the car seats, and our clothes. Bear, unscathed, looked at us and said something like, "Shit, Russ, you better try that one over again."

So, a couple of hours later, I found myself once more standing at a pay phone in the corridor of the Emergency Hospital. "Mom, I'm okay, really. I just broke my nose is all."

It was funny in a way. I'd made it through another night and we were laughing. But I felt death in the air. First James Dean had bought it in his little Porsche Spyder, then my brother, then Patty Wilkerson in U.S. History class who was killed when her boyfriend's TR3 spun out on Skyline Boulevard.

He was a football hero, yet he couldn't hold death off. My brother was tough, a hard guy, nobody messed with him except his girlfriend. But death nailed him on North Delaware Street, floating by like Strontium-90.

So far I'd beat it. But I figured I'd never make it to 30. Like the graffiti said, scrawled on blackboards around San Mateo High that spring: "Live fast, love hard, die young."

Howl of the Baby Beats

One summer afternoon in 1959, three young beats, Ricky Lazaro, Russ Garibaldi, and myself, were heading for San Francisco in Lazaro's prematurely aged '56 Chevy. We were all 17, still living at home in the suburbs, going to the City to pick up some poetry and another thing we couldn't actually name – our code word for it was "reality." Whatever it turned out to be, it was running loose up there, and we were pretty sure we could find it.

I'm the guy with his feet propped on the back of the Chevy's front seat, gazing out its window at cheap motels, brake repair shops and eucalyptus groves skimming along the side of the Bayshore Freeway. The orange striped tail of Pacific Southwest's two o'clock flight from Burbank glided over SFO's chain-link fence. Paul Anka was mewling from the radio about how lonely he was – this was our world, and it wasn't exactly what we had in mind. We wanted to be more like the angelheaded hipsters in Ginsberg's *Howl*, dragging ourselves through San Francisco streets at dawn looking for an angry fix, whatever that meant.

I wasn't sure I could explain *Howl*, Allen Ginsberg's poem comet, but if I'd had to try, I might have brought up our pal Way Out Will Staunton, who'd been thrown out of his parents' designer home again and was sleeping in Bear Ragsdale's '49 Merc.

Way Out was an artist. We figured he'd be famous one day. But there was something skewed about him inside, like that time I knocked over a bust of his girlfriend he had been working on for weeks. It had started out looking like Becky but as the days went on she got older and stranger until she'd become a bust of a queen from Atlantis or somewhere. He'd been sculpting it on the patio, and one evening Russ and I were goofing out there while we waited for him to finish arguing with his sister about some inconsequentiality, and, well, I stumbled against its damn flimsy pedestal and knocked it over and the bust of Queen Becky shattered. Shards skittered into the swimming pool and floated to the bottom.

Way Out didn't react – not at all. He didn't scream at us, didn't cry or laugh, he stayed cool. So cool. One cool hipster cat. But it was uncanny, he should have gotten mad or something. What was going on in there?

I was actually a little skewed myself that summer. Like one night we were at a party at an apartment house over on the El Camino. I had my guitar and was making up a song about how lonely Paul Anka was, mimicking his little boy tenor to big laughs.

But then I actually started to feel lonely and blue and not funny anymore for no reason. I went out the back door and stood by the pool, watching its underwater lights flake through the aquamarine water. I wished a girl would come out and sit beside me and smoke a Kent and not say anything but understand the ice and snow inside me.

There was something wrong in the world. A spirit was loose and he was arrayed against us. Or was it me? I could not have vocalized my turmoil. So instead Russ, and Lazaro and me – we roared up Black Mountain Road, howling past dark Hillsborough mansions. We wrote poetry. We sat around beach party fires in the fog singing "I got a girl lives on the hill, she won't go but her sister will." We got angelheaded drunk and staggering hysterical from dago red in a boda bag

through silent midnight streets walking to Garibaldi's pad for an angry

fix of poetry and jazz because I couldn't get the car tonight.

Man, we wanted to be part of that other, bigger world. But we had to cook some more. Meanwhile, we could roll to San Francisco's North Beach on a summer Sunday afternoon.

The Terrible Truth About Beatniks

While these baby beatniks are rumbling towards fabulous Baghdad-By-The-Bay, its mighty night beacon signaling to freaks and rebels around the world, let us stop to consider exactly what this thing was they wanted to be.

When City Lights Books published *Howl* three years earlier and was busted on obscenity charges, its trial put North Beach on the map. By 1959, everybody who read *Time* magazine knew it was the place to go to see crazy cool free spirits play their bongo drums and smoke their pot and grow their beards and write their obscene poems.

However, the essential thing to know about beatniks is this: there was no such thing. They were a media invention no different than flower power or fill in the relevant hype for your own generation. According to the media, you could tell a beatnik because they wore berets and dark glasses, grew goatees, and snapped their fingers a lot. In fact, beatniks looked like Dizzy Gillespie, who had nothing whatsoever to do with the beat generation, except they probably listened to his records.

There was a beatnik spider in a comic strip who looked a spider version of Dizzy Gillespie, except he was a beatnik. Who knew why? Maybe he spun psychedelic spider webs.

The Hearst Syndicate comic strip characters Jiggs and Maggie gained a beatnik nephew who hung around their house all day, ate sandwiches and wouldn't work. Television offered Maynard G. Krebs, Dobie Gillis's beatnik sidekick who looked and acted just like Archie's pal Jughead, including his big sandwiches and fear of girls.

Day after day, Al Capp's *Li'l Abner* savagely satirized beatniks and peaceniks as stupid but dangerous comsymps (communist sympathizers) out to destroy America for kicks.

Hollywood churned out an epic supposedly based on Jack Kerouac's novel, *The Subterraneans*, but only its title remained when they had finished their story about crooks invading the coffeehouses of North Beach. Mardou Fox, the novel's black heroine from the West Oakland ghetto, was played by Leslie Caron looking waifish in her sad-eyed Parisian beret. Kerouac's character and Leslie Caron became proto-flower children who, in their big scene, bought all the wise old balloon seller's balloons and set them free to soar lyrically past Coit Tower and over sad-eyed waif paintings discarded in the alley behind Finocchio's, a nightclub where tourists could hear singing men dressed like singing women.

After that, crooks crashed the big poetry and jazz session with beatniks snapping their fingers instead of clapping and Roddy McDowell, who they thought was the biggest beatnik of all, turned out to be a crook! And then he tried to blame his crimes on Jack Kerouac! They fought it out in an alley while sad-eyed Leslie Caron looked on in her droopy beret. After that, they got married and went to live in a subdivision in San Mateo.

We watched while the media sucked life from everything we stood for. Except we didn't know what we stood for. But not that!

Actually, the whole sad beatnik circus was good for everybody. It taught us not to trust the media. If they could do this to poor Jack Kerouac and his friends, then what else could they suck the life from to sell newspapers? And it was good for the media too – they got a handy dress rehearsal for their assault on hippies seven years later.

Dig? The Baby Beats weren't real beatniks. But there were no real beatniks, so who cared? What we could do and wanted to do and did do was burn, burn, burn like fabulous yellow Roman candles like they did in *On The Road*. This is not a beatnik aspiration but a human aspiration.

Baby Beatniks In North Beach

So, anyway, we're living big already just by blowin' out of the suburbs and into the city of a million lost hearts' dreams. Lazaro found a place to park on Telegraph Hill and we joy-ran down Filbert Street to Upper Grant, as it was in those last magic moments of the beatnik media frenzy.

First we stood outside the Coffee Gallery listening to Pony Poindexter blowing alto at their Sunday afternoon jam session. The sidewalk was littered with teenagers who wanted to make the scene. Unfortunately, teenaged beatniks were considered a low life form and our flip-flops, sweatshirts and incipient goatees gave us away. The bouncer at the Coffee Gallery was a good guy, though, and left us alone unless we kept paying customers from the door.

Actually, Lazaro, in his baggy brown wool actor's sweater, didn't dig jazz that much – maybe it didn't leave enough room for his expansive personality. Big long lined poetry was more his style, especially if he could declaim it at parties to peals of laughter. But he loved North Beach – he planned on moving to a bohemian hotel there, as soon as he could afford it, and painting and starving for up to a week.

Garibaldi was silent, but you could tell from his eyes he was thinking, "Yeah man! Go! Go!" as we whirled our eyes up and down the street to see how older cats portrayed coolness. I liked music in all forms from Little Richard to Prokofieff, but at the moment rock and roll was filled with pretty boy pretenders like Paul Anka. Jazz seemed to be the key to the future and we needed to fill our heads with as much as we could.

Grant Avenue was crowded with happy Sunday afternoon tourists, not a bit like us of course, heading downhill towards the nightclubs on Broadway. Paddy O'Sullivan stood at the corner of Grant and Columbus, dressed like one of the Three Musketeers in high boots and a plume-feathered hat, hawking his book of poems.

Some "in" person told us he hadn't written them at all; he'd stolen them from some big New York poet. I doubted it, though. Stealing somebody's poems, then printing them in a little book with his name on it – too much work. Besides, why steal from somebody who might notice? He could have printed up Percy Bysshe Shelley's stuff and sold it as his own.

It was a gag anyway, right? Who cared if he was a real poet? He was great, a San Francisco character like Emperor Norton or Oofty Goofty of long-ago Barbary Coast times. Tourists surrounded him, listening excitedly to Paddy's spiel.

Oh Upper Grant Avenue of the summer of 1959, street of swimming crowds and cool daddy-ohs and remittance men in abstract residence hotels and dusty Figoni's hardware store selling screwdrivers next to the Italian-French Bakery of anise crunch delight. The beatniks and the tourists and the elderly Italian men walking out to smoke their evil-smelling rope cigars, and the dogs trotting freely in the street, and the pigeons waiting to be marked, and the Chinese ladies off to work at their sewing machines, and Mimi and Rudolfo falling in love in their garret above the Caffe Trieste – all on a sunny Sunday before school began and I blew out of town to San Jose State to start my college career.

We ducked across the street and hustled up a block to The Scene, an art gallery next to Gene Wright's photography studio, its window filled with black and white images of cable cars disappearing into fog. It was always closed. But The Scene was open, and we liked to go in there because – they had no good reason to keep us out.

In the Caffe Trieste, the in-est coffee house on the Beach, we could stand at its counter for hours, but good luck getting served. Intelligent businessmen, they had a vested interest in keeping suburban 17-year-old riffraff thinned out.

Mike's Pool Hall? Its worldly denizens would have a good laugh if we tried racking up the balls. After the laugh, out the door! We were fleas and disease – even if we were the future. That's why we liked The Scene. We could look around as long as we wanted. The beautiful black-haired shop girl, she didn't care. There was nothing in the shop we could steal.

There were art galleries at home in San Mateo, of course. Their paintings featured waves breaking at twilight with glimmers of green as a duck drops down. But The Scene's window presented gray and mauve paint slathered on canvas with a palette knife, the colors sliding into each other so you couldn't see where they met. I thought I saw a robot shape in tan outlined in black, frozen in gray-mauve gloom. That was great!

Inside were paintings like what psychotics might make in art therapy – stuff even I could recognize were great personal nightmares but terrible art, yet they hung on the same wall with the gray-mauve palette knife paintings.

The yet greater attraction of The Scene was the beatnik chick sitting bored at its counter. She had thick black hair with bangs and a ponytail and mascara, lots and lots of mascara and layered eye shadow – the careful drama that makes a nice Jewish girl from Brooklyn look Egyptian, exotic and beyond all reach forever.

She wore a black sweater and a tight skirt with black tights beneath. And she stood out from the paintings like Cleopatra visiting a mental ward. Lazaro wasn't that interested in girls, but Russ and I studied the art while stealing looks at this goddess come to our own North Beach. She ignored us, yet there she is today, emerging clear on my eyelid screen, still perched on her stool behind the glass counter, reading Camus, burgundy lipstick smudged on the tip of her Winston.

But you know where else we were welcome in spite of our sweatshirts and flip-flops and hopeful goatee wisps and itchy fingers? City Lights, the legendary bookstore and meeting place at the corner of Broadway and Columbus. City Lights had everything we needed to prepare for our journey into hipness – a passage that would get us a table at the Caffe

21

Trieste and Vesuvio's and Mike's Pool Hall and maybe even the Co-Existence Bagel Shop.

I liked going down its narrow, winding stairs into the poetry cellar because on the right, before the stairs made their turn, Lawrence Ferlinghetti had nailed a bulletin board. Scanning notebook scraps from hipsters looking for a ride to New York or wanting to share expenses for an apartment in the Fillmore or about an upcoming event at the Poetry Center, it was heady – a window through which I could see real people living the life Kerouac encouraged us to live through his books. (That was actually the last thing he intended to do, but he wrote about his time and place too well.)

Continuing down the stairs, we emerged into the cellar, with its collection of literary journals from around the world – *Big Table, Evergreen Review, Paris Review*, and – the hottest item on any beatnik's list – *Beatitude,* the mimeographed sheet put out by Pierre DeLattre's Bread and Wine Mission, up the hill on the corner of Grant and Greenwich. Browsing in the cellar was like walking into a great conversation between all the hippest, most creative people you could never meet in ordinary teenage life. And you could sit there as long as you wanted, you and your pals, browsing, checking them out, and if you found something you really liked, stealing it!

What brats! Why did we do that? Why did we bite the hand that fed us?

We would never steal from a friend – but Lawrence Ferlinghetti? No problem! If I had been caught and eighty-sixed from the store, or worse, I would have been devastated. But for some reason I don't understand now but understood then, stolen poetry tasted better.

Did we think we were anarchist Abomunists? I'm sure we didn't understand we were no different than any other shoplifter who can afford to buy the product. We saw it, we wanted it, and we figured we could get away with it. Simple and ugly. (The trouble with all this deep memory is now I have to write a check to City Lights for ancient poetry thefts.)

Night is falling as the Baby Beats emerge from City Lights with treasures they didn't walk in with stuffed in their shirts. They head up Broadway to a deli on the corner of Kearney and emerge with their beat supper of French rolls, dry salami, and a quart of milk each. They walk past Mike's Pool Hall in jubilant spirits, hike high up Russian Hill and sit on a concrete balustrade looking over the twilight city. The neon lights of Broadway are just switching on, the girl who dances in a cage above the entrance to Gorman's Gay Nineties is getting out of her taxi, and bouncers are sweeping the sidewalks. Beyond the streets the Bay Bridge glows in the fading sunset light. Oh, what a beautiful city San Francisco is.

Baby Beats

San Jose, San Francisco, On The Road,

San Miguel de Allende, Manhattan

1959-62

My Joe College Year

It was still sweltering on the lawns of San Jose State, as it is across much of California in mid-September. Bobbi Monticello and I sat side by side at the Walgreen's lunch counter on East Santa Clara Street, perspiring and trading jokes about the snaking registration lines we'd just finished gasping through. Bobbi was a luscious brunette from San Mateo High, same as me (although I wasn't a luscious brunette). Like freshman kids all over the country who knew each other from high school, we were huddling together for a few weeks, dabbling our toes in the waters of college life and getting ready to jump in.

Bobbi was a drama major; I was going to study English. We had nothing in common except familiarity and comfort and mutual friends and shared memories, and that was plenty. Besides, she was a major babe. Frat-rat heads swiveled to watch her walk by. She'd have impressed the heck out of my friends, if I'd had any yet – besides Bobbi. We drank root beer from Coke glasses and munched tuna sandwiches on white bread with a side of potato salad on half a lettuce leaf and a pickle slice. I wasn't Beat today, I was trying out Joe College.

San Jose State was great for trying on that role. It had its share of concrete buildings designed for maximum boxy cheapness, but it also had Tower Hall, a vine-encrusted brick building from 1910, when philosophy and art still mattered.

To me, Tower Hall exhaled perfume from a richer time, when A. E. Housman and F. Scott Fitzgerald and other earnest thinkers devoted their lives to the Big Eternal questions. I could dawdle along its ivy-covered arcades and listen to the buzz of droning professors through propped-open classroom doors. I could hear them lecturing on Intermediate Latin, Continental Literature, Bonehead English, and it made me sleepy. I lay me down under a jacaranda tree and took my rest.

I dreamed I was living in the 1920s, wearing a tight sweater and floppy bell-bottom trousers and smoking a pipe like Bing Crosby and I fell in love with the Latin professor's daughter. Beneath the San Jose moon, I serenaded her from inside the rosebush where I was hiding but when she strolled onto the balcony to hear my throbbing tenor voice more clearly, I rushed out and declared my love forever, but then her father, who had a long white beard and spectacles, chased me around the rosebush shouting, "You're not good enough, you're not good enough!" until he fell on his butt.

But then he laughed and forgave me because he was a good fellow after all beneath his gruff exterior and he decided I was good enough after all and my fraternity brothers jumped out from the rosebushes to sing harmony, but then his virginal daughter with flowing blonde locks decided she liked the football hero who was singing the ooh-bop-she-bop part better than she liked me and she married him and left me alone to suffer and die in a ratty hotel with pee stains on my underwear even though I was Good Enough.

That was me, creating my own universe as I went along, but most guys at San Jose State preferred to take their reality straight.

Here come some now. It must be lunchtime because they are walking in a tough engineering student gang down Seventh Street toward the student cafeteria. You can tell they're engineering students because they all wear butchwaxed flattops and tan chinos. They keep sturdy plastic pocket protectors jammed in their madras shirt pockets, and from their pocket protectors they whip out their slide rules to make quick calculations as they walk. I figure they're arguing over how many angels can dance on the head of a pin.

It was a different time, the fall of 1959 – for one thing, girls still went to college to get their MRS degree. They majored in home ec or phys ed or elementary ed and waited for the magic to happen and good luck and God bless them. They didn't see any joke about it. They were in the market for a successful husband, and San Jose State was the market.

Here come a gaggle of them now. (You're probably asking why guys walk in gangs, but girls walk in gaggles. It's because I have my sexist 1959 eyes on, okay?) Note their tight plaid skirts and white blouses. Except Ponytail One is wearing a sleeveless dress with petticoats beneath it in spite of the heat. Actually, they're kind of cute in their poodle cuts and ducktails and ponytails. And is their lipstick red! They're on their way to the student cafeteria too, to listen to "Running Bear loved little White Dove" on the jukebox and glance semi-casually at the dorky engineering students.

Then Paul Anka is going to sing "Hold me in your arms bay-bey, maybe you and I will fall in love."

Sometimes hunger would drag me into the cafeteria and force me to witness these mating rituals. But mostly the cool people (which included me, of course) stopped in about 4 o'clock when the place was nearly empty. Then I could put Oscar Peterson and Chet Baker on the jukebox to play "Round About Midnight" and "Angel Eyes." Running Bear would have to meet Little White Dove somewhere else. Yes, one cool thing about 1959 was that jazz and rock and roll could cohabit the jukebox comfortably together. Like they did inside my head. And I could drink coffee and write in my journal and wonder if somewhere on campus there was a beautiful Baby Beat girl for me.

You remember Bobbi Monticello? My friend at the top of the story? Bobbi wasn't a gumsnapper like those coeds walking down the street. She was my friend and those other girls weren't, so even if she didn't really like jazz or know anything about Jack Kerouac, she was still cool, okay?

29

Yesterday, we both stood in line in sun that made our heads ache for hours waiting to get our registration packets. The sophomores, juniors and seniors – they had theirs, all right. They were already inside the gym, racing from table to table, signing up for whatever they wanted. Once all the classes were full, then they let the freshmen in.

But we won in the end. We had classes too, even if they weren't exactly what we'd planned on. I even got my English 3A class, required of and dreaded by freshman English majors. That's the class where I was taught, once and for all, when I was writing a paper, not to ramble. I was to grab hold of that theme and shake it like a rat terrier shakes a rat.

We had new homes too. Bobbi moved into the girl's dorms and I checked into a boarding house on South Twelfth. Of course we would never see each other's rooms. She could welcome me into her dorm lobby with all the other girls and their dates but not one step further. And my landlady, Mrs. O'Reilly, would have had a heart attack if a *girl* had knocked on her front door asking to see one of the guys. The adult world knew what young people would get up to if they were left alone for even a minute, and they were going to make damn sure they never were.

Of course, no one considered what two guys might get up to if left alone in their room together. This was 1959. "Gay" meant "cheerful." Of course there were *homos* and *queers* out there somewhere, but they didn't go to San Jose State. I figured homosexuals were mostly paunchy middle-aged men with psychological problems who lived in San Francisco's Polk Gulch.

My roomie was a big older guy majoring in police science. He never smiled. His dad was the chief of police in one of the San Joaquin Valley farm towns. I might creep back at 3 a.m. from some horrible drunken debauch to find him still up studying. We didn't have much to talk about, but one Sunday he invited me to go with him to the Baptist church he attended out in Los Gatos. And I, with great nonchalance, agreed to check it out. I might learn something.

I didn't know what to expect. My parents, when they went to church at all, were of the polite and proper Episcopal persuasion. For me, church happened in Gothic stone buildings that should be in an Agatha Christie mystery, with bald fellows in white cassocks who handed out communion wafers at the altar rail with real wine in little shot glasses, and it was steeped in a thousand years of ritual and was peaceful and soothing and kind of spiritual in a funny way. I'd never stepped inside a Baptist church.

Not that I wasn't worldly. By 17 I was pretty damn sophisticated. I knew the score, man. Why, in high school I had written a poem that began:

Man is lost on a moor
Blind and deaf and lost on a moor.

Ha ha! Let us laugh and be gay in the face of this bitter, tragic joke of life! Then I would light my pipe and stride gloomily into the mist, keeping careful watch for the Hound of the Baskervilles.

So we drove out to Los Gatos. Before I knew it, the preacher had launched into his sermon about why Caryl

Chessman should be executed. This was a major case at the time, and awareness of it had even dribbled down to apolitical 17-year-olds like me. Chessman was, supposedly, the notorious "Red Light Bandit" who had robbed and raped women in L.A. many years before. He was still on Death Row, but time was running out for him. Even proponents of capital punishment felt the case was unsettling, because Chessman – if it was Chessman – hadn't actually been accused of killing anyone.

The preacher thought Chessman should be executed because he had violated God's law and God was a real stickler for punishing anybody who disobeyed him. The pastor went right through the Old Testament, pointing out how this kind of miscreant was stoned and how women were supposed to be stoned too, if they helped their husbands in a fight by grabbing the bad guy's balls and squeezing real hard.

Well, maybe he didn't actually mention that one. Some stuff in the Bible wasn't even proper for Baptists.

Even young guys like me who disobeyed their parents were stoned, and pretty soon my blood was running cold and I was getting mad. What kind of God did these people believe in? And how can I get out of here without causing a scene?

I figured, "Well, this guy is a preacher so he must know what he's talking about. But if the Bible really says things like that, then it's just one more proof that God isn't real because if there really is a God, no way would he say things like that."

We drove home in cool silence. Next semester, I moved in with a history major from Castro Valley who smoked a pipe and knew who Federico Fellini was.

It didn't take long for the Joe College thing to wear off. Where was the romance of college life? I was disillusioned. Take my boarding house, for instance. It was classic: a Queen Anne Victorian with a wraparound veranda. Wisteria climbed the pillars and its purple flowers dripped amorous perfume. Theoretically, I should be able to relax on the porch swing, play my guitar and sing Ricky Nelson songs, and pretty soon coeds would gather round and swoon, like they did in the perfect 1925 of my imagination – except if it was 1925 I'd be playing a ukulele.

But our landlady, Mrs. O'Leary, must have sprinkled Coed Powder around the perimeter of the place, because none ever showed up or even walked by. The only student who stopped to listen was the accounting major who lived on the second floor. And he mainly wanted to show me again how he could play "Rebel Rouser," a twangy guitar hit from a few months before. Of course, it lost much of its twangy sound when attempted on my Japanese nylon string. And since he'd only had four lessons, I wouldn't have known it *was* "Rebel Rouser" except he told me.

I was already getting tired of eating breakfast every morning with the other boarders. Like the business major who made fun of the way I ate my fried eggs. Whenever I dabbed my toast into the yolk, this guy would pretend to scream in pain. It was funny, I guess, but it wasn't funny every morning. I tried to remember that he was just another poor sap, destined for a life of tedium in the suburbs while I was living in Greenwich Village having a great time.

There was one bright light at Mrs. O'Leary's boarding house, though – a rock and roll teenager from the San Fernando Valley named Bill Kaplan. Most kids, when they got to college, traded in their teenager image as fast as they could, but Bill wore his like a badge of honor. Nothing about San Jose State could compare with the mythic grandeur of Van Nuys High, his alma mater.

Bill was a natural storyteller, and endlessly entertaining. We would gather in his room and pretty soon he would conjure up '56 Chevy convertibles and Corvettes and '49 Mercs cruising down Ventura Boulevard on perfumed nights while guys in D.A.'s or flattops insulted each other and peeled out. His world wasn't that different from the one we had just escaped from, but he was a better storyteller than any of us. His stories were filled with teen angels and tragedy and Romeo and Juliet with a ponytail. We had to know what happened next.

In his stories, Van Nuys High was a miniature Peyton Place. Take the story about the time his friends Chuck and Connie broke up. Chuck didn't take it well, especially when right away Connie started going steady with Chuck's rival. One night, Chuck was pulling out of the burger joint when he saw the new couple making out in Chuck's rival's Corvette. Chuck unrolled his window, looked over and called out so everyone could hear, "Hey, man, you just kissed the lips that sucked my dick."

The guys sitting around Bill's room, including me, were staggered. We gasped, we cheered. That was the best putdown any of us had ever heard! There was going to be one helluva fight for sure, or maybe a grudge drag race up Mulholland Drive with somebody's loaded '34 Ford tum-bling end over end over the cliff and exploding in flames into the crashing waves beneath. And Bill would be right there with the heart-pounding details.

Whether he was telling us about drag strip riots, or the time his friends were lighting farts and caught the curtains on fire, Bill's stories had conflict and character development and punch lines. Who knew when he left strict reality behind? Who cared? Did he really take Annette Funicello to his prom? I half believed he did. He *was* from a show business family. He told me his father wrote "You Never Miss the Water till the Well Runs Dry," and he said it as if I should be impressed. So I was.

Bill never bothered to study and he never looked at girls. He was engaged to a honeybabe Valley girl back home and longed for her embrace. Every night he'd walk to the phone booth up on Santa Clara Street to hear her honeyed voice again. He just wanted to get back to the San Fernando Valley as soon as he could and marry that girl.

I couldn't understand it myself, but I decided he showed heart. There it was, right where I could see it – true love. I watched him through the phone booth glass and wished I had a girl like that.

Once, after his Honey call, we walked downtown to see the new Sandra Dee flick, *Gidget*. Bill told me he knew most of the actors and maybe he did, maybe he didn't. I never was quite sure, but I learned a lot about story-telling from him.

Bill lasted one semester, then got his wish, flunked out and went home. I never saw him again, but I've often wondered if he married that honeybabe and if he got into show business like his father. Once I even looked him up on the Internet Movie Database. It did show somebody with his name had directed porn in the Seventies. Could it have been him? Did he and Honey live in a big house in the San Fernando Valley, and did he go off to his job directing hot sex scenes all day, then come home and read his kids a bedtime story? It was slightly possible, but I hoped he didn't.

Yet Another Reason Not To Smoke

One night in the summer of 1960, the Baby Beats – Bear Ragsdale, Way Out Will Staunton, Ricky Lazaro, Russ Garibaldi and myself – are driving around San Mateo in Bear's '49 Merc, wondering what to do with the night. The Merc's radio is on, and they're being treated to another encore of the moment's Top 40 smash, "Alley Oop" ("He's the king of the jungle jive, look at that caveman go").

Russ shouts from the back seat, "Hey Willy, change the station, will you? My ears hurt." But the other Top 40 provider is spewing up worse, an angelic tenor sobbing out misery because his steady girl, Mary Lou Crumpleton, crawled back into the car to retrieve his high school ring just before the locomotive hit and sent her winging to paradise and they buried her today and he's so fucked up he can't even play rock and roll but instead is strumming ONE two three four ONE two three four like Mrs. O'Elderlee showed him in his guitar lesson and now he's just going to go home and eat vanilla ice cream with Hershey syrup after he's made us all sick to our stomachs and maybe we should go to emergency and get our ears pumped.

At least "Alley Oop" had that backbeat you can't lose it. And the song included a dinosaur, which was unusual.

Kids, this was the dark night of rock and roll. All the madness-inducing outlaw beats, the glorious chromatics of street-corner doo-wop, all gone. Elvis was in the Army, Buddy Holly in his sudden grave, Jerry Lee Lewis in jail, and Little Richard now a man of the cloth. The Beatles were still four years in the future. Squeamishness, mawkishness, and mayonnaise have won the day. FM car radios haven't hit yet, so there's no cool jazz in the air for leftover beats who might still be cruising the summer night.

In these real life American Graffiti summer nights of 1960, the Baby Beats got home just before dawn, having gone nowhere and done nothing. They'd spent another night roaming and roaming, looking for a party, looking for someone to buy them beer, driving to San Francisco and walking around North Beach, Telegraph Hill, Chinatown, then back to San Mateo, rambling from The Weasel's house to Mickey's house to Buzzy's house to see what was up, but nothing ever was. They invented songs (often obscene, always funny) and made each other laugh. And just really dug being together. Pals, you know? They weren't bored at all. In fact, it was a perfect life.

On this particular night, it's still early, sometime before midnight. Rounding the corner from Palm Avenue onto Ninth, Newton asks Bear if he can borrow a smoke. Bear hands it over and Newt puts a match to it.

Unfortunately, he's forgotten he has a wad of surgical cotton in his nose. He's been having trouble with nosebleeds; a doc cauterized the problem vein that afternoon and told him to leave the cotton in overnight.

So, when he lights the Camel, his nose lights too. The Baby Beats turn and stare. Is this a gag to get more laughs? A fire on Newt's nose! If so, it works pretty well.

Newt, though, is not laughing. "I don't think this is funny, okay?" he says. There is a seeping pink welt where his skin used to be.

Bear suggests it might be wise to get Newt to Emergency before gangrene sets in. So the Merc rumbles to life again. They roar around the corner onto the main drag and head north toward the hospital – about 50 feet, then the street rod sputters and stops dead. They're out of gas.

After a hasty conference, they decide the best plan is to push the Merc seven blocks to the Chevron station on Second Avenue.

They do eventually get to the hospital – pushing that big Merc entire seven blocks. Fortunately, they have a dollar between them for three gallons of gas. Then Newt has to call his parents again. "Mom, I'm at the Emergency Hospital. But I'm okay! Really! It's only a second-degree burn."

The Bus Ride Home

I was going to be a writer when I grew up, an important novelist like Jack Kerouac. My plan was to hitchhike everywhere, love all the longhaired beatnik chicks, grow up to live in Greenwich Village and write about the exciting things that had happened to me. You must admit it's not a bad plan. I'd do what I wanted to do anyway and make a living at it.

I never wondered if I'd be happy. Happiness was not part of the equation.

One December night on the Greyhound bus creeping back up the Peninsula from San Jose State to San Mateo for the weekend, I started thinking about my friend Way Out Willy, who was sleeping in Bear Ragsdale's car because his parents had thrown him out. I didn't know why.

I wanted to write about stuff like that too. I could make a story out of it. What if I was on a bus like this one, but I'd been on the road for weeks and weeks and I was burnt out, gone, exhausted in heart and soul? What if I was dragging my weary ass back to my hometown even though my parents were dead or somewhere, but a heartsick longing compelled me home across the snowy continent anyway? Suppose I knew when I got to my best friend Way Out's house (hmm, I'd have to give him another name) I would be welcomed like a son, received into the warmth of his family, be fed and a have real bed to sleep in. I'd be safe to heal.

So, in my story dream, the Greyhound grumbled to a stop at the B Street bus depot on a rainy Christmas night and I limped through darkened downtown streets with only an occasional lighted Santa Claus statuette in a window to illuminate my backpack and worn 17-year-old face. I stumbled up wet winding roads through Hillsborough's shuttered mansions and on into the subdivisions on the hill's crest. The diamond pinpoints of Peninsula suburban towns glittered far below.

I hobbled up Crestview Drive, past spidery glass-walled homes, so contemporary, so carefree, so success-oriented. As I approached Way Out's place, still hidden by the night, I heard angry voices. Way Out's father stood silhouetted in the doorway. He was shouting at Will and Will was just standing there, taking it. Next he heaved Will's paintings and sculptures into the rain and kept shouting until Will's best stuff lay sodden in the grass, rain showering on his portrait of our friend Gypsy Girl, raindrop tears puddling on her dark cheeks. The door slammed shut, leaving Way Out standing in the rain in his Levi's and red windbreaker in the *Rebel Without A Cause* night.

So I said, "Hey, man."

And Willy saw me and he said, "Hey man."

Then we just stood there because we didn't know where to go or what else to say.

That was the real truth – even if it never happened. I had to write about kids lost and loose on the sorrowful Crestview Drive of time.

The hard part to being a famous writer, or any kind of writer really, was that I had to sit at a typewriter for a long time every day. And I had to sweat and sweat until I got an idea. And then I had to write sentences that described something hidden away inside me where I couldn't see it, let alone understand it.

And then the words on the page usually sounded stupid when I read them to myself out loud, and I had to throw the whole thing out and start over. All that work for nothing.

Then there was the part where I walked around and wouldn't talk to anybody and people thought I was sulking when I was just trying to find the right place in my head. Where is it? It was there yesterday!

I wasn't really reconciled to the writer life.

Singing and playing guitar were so much easier and so much more fun. I got instant feedback when friends laughed at my lyrics and girls at parties looked at me with big eyes. I never stressed over it – just rock and roll. I never felt that secret fear I might not really be one of the greats.

But somebody had to tell our damned story. No one else was!

So I'm doing it now.

Getting My Ticket Punched, Part I

By the spring of 1960, I had acquired a cute blonde high school senior named Gail. Figuratively speaking, we danced the bop at the hop and once, after Grad Night, we parked under the Golden Gate Bridge and necked until dawn. I was hot for her and she was hot for me. But, toward the end of the year, she decided to dump me for a guy who pumped gas at the all night station in Millbrae. He said he wanted to marry her, she was so cute, and she was, and they did.

I stood in the January 1961 rain on Coyote Point Beach, brokenhearted, pissed off, wet, and watching DC-8s glide over the bay through my bitter tears. What was the point? Why was I pretending to myself I wanted to become a rich Hollywood screenwriter and live in a fancy house in Sea Cliff gazing at the Golden Gate Bridge through the picture window of my mink-lined prison while sea lions barked and gulls wept? That was Gail's dream, not mine. Why should I live in someone else's dream? Screw that! While mist swirled through the eucalyptus trees, I decided on a life of adventure.

Instead of going home, I drove up to Bear Ragsdale's house in the hills above San Mateo. His greasy jeans and horseshoe-tapped shoes were sticking out from under his '49 Merc.

"Hey Bear! Let's go to Mexico."

"Huh? What? Wait a minute." He scraped himself from under the jacked-up Merc and sat up. Grease was smeared across his forehead. His dirty blond hair, falling in his eyes, stuck in it.

It wasn't that weird of an idea. Will Staunton had gone to art school in San Miguel de Allende the preceding summer, then hitchhiked to Manzanillo and back. He returned with a photo of himself tanned and blond-bearded in a cowboy hat with an artist chick on his arm. We could do the same thing. We had a precedent.

Bear laid down his grease gun, pulled his Ronson lighter from his shirt pocket and lit a Camel.

"You serious?"

"Yeah, let's go." Pretty soon we were talking about how we could pull it off. Bear had seen a '49 Willys panel truck for sale for $250. I was short on cash but could get a few bucks for my old Chevy. That would pay for my half of the truck plus travel expenses and tuition at the *Instituto*. Bear thought he might go to art school there too. We had to give our parents some plausible excuse.

So instead of registering for spring semester, I dropped out of San Jose State, Bear quit the College of San Mateo, and, one morning in late February 1961, we rumbled down the Bayshore Freeway toward beckoning Mexico.

Somewhere near Bakersfield we picked up our first hitchhiker, a sandy-haired hobo who was heading east somewhere, not sure where, glad to be out of the cold. Sitting by our first campfire, under a Joshua tree on the edge of the Mojave, he showed us how to roll Bull Durham cigarettes from the ungummed papers that came with the pouch so they stuck together long enough to smoke. He wasn't much of a talker, but that was okay. I got out my guitar and sang a few tunes, hoping to make the coyotes howl.

In the morning, leftover coffee had frozen into black crystals in the bottom of our pot. We crossed the sere Mojave, jackets zipped, collars turned up, contemplating bleak creosote bushes stretching toward the Granite Mountains. Bear was driving, so I retrieved a book from my pack, poetry by somebody named Wallace Stevens. I didn't know much about him, except he had been famous back in the Twenties and people were still reading him.

I sat on my sleeping roll, flipped through the book, settled on a poem called "Sunday Morning," and started up my poetry engine. I didn't get far. Damn! I'd been hoping for wild flying riffs, but it turned out I needed a jeweler's eyeglass and hadn't brought one along.

I'd read T. S. Eliot in high school so I recognized the style. He was all about sitting quietly in a perfect room examining delicate filigree while servants hovered. Maybe he'd shoot out an illumination at the end, and maybe he wouldn't. Patience and serenity, that's what I needed, but neither quality had been handed through the watchmaker's window.

I wasn't so arrogant as to think that I knew what was happening and Wallace Stevens didn't. I felt ignorant and wished I wasn't. I couldn't grasp "Sunday Morning," couldn't explain it, couldn't interpret it or anything else, really. I looked out at the scabby desert country and wondered if April's green could really endure, like he said in his poem, or had I completely misunderstood him?

We crossed the Mojave and then the vast Sonoran Desert on solitary two-lane highways. We camped in the Vulture Mountains, watched buzzards wheeling in the early dusk. We shoveled homemade chili beans Bear's mother had canned for us.

Next day we stopped in Tucson to see Weasel Williams, who was at the university because it was supposed to be a party school. Weasel was rushing a fraternity. We had nothing to say to each other. We didn't stay long. I made a note: "I hate college. I want to go to school."

That night we camped in Sabino Canyon, just Bear and me in the icy night. We'd bought a pork steak in town, built a campfire, laid our oven rack over it on some stones. Bear threw on the steak, I mixed a pot full of cowboy coffee for later, then sat on a rock as night came down, watching Bear blow on little bits and drip water on other little bits.

My mind was still running on Wallace Stevens' poem.

"So Bear, what I figure is if you take any important-sounding thought and dig around inside it long enough, it will turn to dust. You might as well knock your ear right now and shake that thought out. It will yield nothing. Nothing, man."

"Okay. So?"

"So look at the creek, that fire. They're real, right? But geometry or existentialism, or even God, they're just ideas. If there was a trout in that stream, it would be a *real* trout."

"You know what I think? I think this steak is done."

Bear was a good friend but not much interested in big ideas before dinner. I puzzled and puzzled and grew more confused until I'd forgotten what my question was, let alone found an answer. Side roads where the obvious turned obscure opened at every turn. Horrible paradoxes leered through the brush.

We washed dishes, huddled by the remnants of the fire, and then the sleeping bags. Under the moon, a raccoon ate my gloves.

Next day we stopped on the border to buy Mexican insurance for the truck. Before we left home, we had been warned: "You hit a cow in that thing and you can't pay up, they'll throw your ass in jail."

We didn't know if it was true, but neither one of us wanted to find out. So we bought enough insurance to get to San Miguel. Then we crossed our fingers and crossed the border into Nogales.

Curio shops lined the streets, offering piñatas, painted pots and crap like that. We stopped in some place with a name like El Exquisito and ordered beers. This part was good. We had just bought two bottles of Carta Blanca for 16 cents American and now we were drinking them peaceful as you please. Nobody was checking the birthdate on our drivers' licenses because drinking Carta Blanca in a cafe on Tourisma Street was perfectly legal for 18-year-old guys. We scanned the menu. We weren't sure exactly what an enchilada was, but at least we'd heard of it, so we ordered two and they were good.

As we stepped out of the cafe, a taxi driver wondered if we might like to visit some pretty ladies, and it turned out we did. I was suspicious of the guy, but it was true, I wanted to visit some pretty ladies and so did Bear. The casa de putas was a mile or two outside Nogales, in a broken-down hacienda surrounded by cottonwood trees and mesquite. If we got dumped, we'd never find our way back.

Inside was a bar, a couple of guys sitting at it, maybe other cab drivers – and a row of pretty ladies. Well, maybe not exactly pretty ladies, but they *were* girls. One of them grabbed me by the arm. She was young and chubby. And in a hurry; those little cubicles behind the cantina were cold. She refused to even take off her blouse.

"Oh, *chico*, faster, faster!"

Our cabbie barely had time to down a Carta Blanca.

The cabbie silently returned us to town, we found our Willys, then headed through the night towards Guaymas, no older, maybe a little wiser. At least they hadn't rolled us.

Somewhere in the Sinaloa farmlands, the clutch crapped out. We made camp by the side of the road. We despaired, we laughed, despaired again, laughed again. We ate cold tamales from a can. In the morning we flagged down a pickup truck full of crazy guys. For a hundred pesos, they towed us thirty miles to Guamúchil, where there was supposed to be a garage.

The garage turned out to be a corrugated iron roof over a dirt floor, decorated with a collection of wrecked cars awaiting reincarnation. We couldn't see where their business came from, since only donkey carts roamed the streets.

It turned out people don't need to speak the same language to repair cars together. Bear laughed and growled and shared his Camels and pretty soon the Mexican car guys knew exactly what he needed and, amazingly, found a clutch plate that fit. Villagers stood watching. I found the *excusado*, but there was no water and no clean toilet paper. Plenty of the used stuff, though, in a box next to the toilet. I walked around the village and wrote in my journal in the shade, while Bear sweated under the truck. I would have helped if I could but I knew nothing about cars. It was embarrassing.

On the road - Spring, 1961

I watched a kitten cross the counter of the *refresco* stand. Señora waved it off. Outside the cantina, a chicken pecked a bug. I could hear Bear swearing in English under the truck.

South of Culiacan, a rear tire blew. We jacked up the back, took off the tire, patched the tube, pumped it 400 times, replaced the tire, jumped in the truck, drove 10 miles and it blew again. Ten miles further on, it blew again. We rolled that way for 150 miles through the tropical rain forest, past thatched roof villages, Fanta stands and veiled darkness. In a clearing, we suddenly saw a brightly lit cabana, filled with pool tables. Hombres in white suits and straw cowboy hats stood scowling into the night.

We patched that raw tire all the way to Mazatlán. We camped in the dark on an empty beach north of the city and woke to see green islands a quarter mile out, so beautiful.

The tire shop was closed. Of course it would be closed, it was Sunday. We didn't care. We drove through the city, slowing whenever we saw a group of dark-haired maidens strolling together. We would ask them for directions just to connect for a minute, so charming, so modest, yet so sexy in their sleeveless spring dresses. They laughed at us gringo boys and pointed in all directions, and we laughed too.

Back at camp, we broke open coconuts that had washed onto the beach and bodysurfed through tropical waves.

Monday morning we bought a tire, then rolled through mosquito-infested banana plantations to the sea at San Blas, drank too many beers in the cantina, then next day over mountain passes to Guadalajara.

We spotted a go-kart track on the edge of the city and spent a lazy hour racing around it at 15 miles per hour, same as we did back home. Bear's big bear body crammed into a go-kart built for a 12-year-old, lanky hair falling in face, grease in knuckles from changing the clutch plate, big mitts wrapped around the mini-steering wheel, pedal to the metal, Camel between his lips, laughing and growling as he prevented me or anybody else from getting past him. We were in our comfort zone again, just for a moment. Then we groaned over further turista-prone mountains to the expat artist colony at San Miguel de Allende.

Life was good there, even if, within some, some drunken young guys dropped a lighted cigarette in the rear of the van and our gear smelled like it had been marinated in burning plastic. I fell in with a beat from Kansas who looked amazingly like Maynard G. Krebs, and an artist from Manitoba who strolled through town with a parrot perched on his shoulder. I learned to carry a staff to threaten off marauding dog packs.

I fell under the spell of an artist from Brooklyn named Layla Kaplan, dark and mysterious. She tied her lustrous hair in a ponytail, wore handmade sandals and had made the scene in Quintana Roo. She was wise and I was not but she liked me anyway. If I met her in the morning for *café con leche*, I was king of the rest of my day. Sadly, she was married.

I joined the expat writers' group and met a guy named Walter Tevis who'd sold his first novel to the movies and Jackie Gleason was going to star in it. Tevis was wandering Mexico with his family while he waited for the film to begin production in Hollywood. He read my stories and told me I could do things on paper he never could. After that, I was his admirer and defender.

Then I met an angelic Italian teenager whose parents had sent him off to Mexico because he was gay, and a scandal. He invited me to move in with him, but I liked girls and I knew it would only lead to heartbreak, not mine. But he was so pretty! I'd never met a guy before who wore a flower in his hair. Of course, later they'd be plentiful.

One night after I'd had a few too many *Cuba Libres* in La Cucaracha, a sentimental local drinking buddy decided we should be buddies forever. We'd seal the deal by exchanging rings. He handed me his precious wedding ring, which split in half three days later, and I handed him my lusted-after high school class ring with its gleaming black stone and the words *Semper Fidelis Bearcats* embossed in something gold-colored. Of course I never saw the jerk again, but why'd he want my class ring? In my innocence, I couldn't figure it out. If he wanted it, just ask, he didn't have to scam me – I wanted nothing further to do with the world that ring represented. That phase was over, man. Overdue to be over.

At the *Instituto*, I fell in love with an intense 20-year-old from Shaker Heights, Ohio, named Janice. Her pushy grandmother had hauled her off to bohemian San Miguel de Allende after tracking down Janice in the Village in the midst of an affair with Charles Mingus. She couldn't care less that

Mingus was a jazz great. He was a Negro, and "nice" people in Shaker Heights didn't have love affairs with Negros.

I knew all about Charles Mingus, of course. We used to play *Blues & Roots* in Russ Garibaldi's living room after school, and when I learned she'd been balling him, her desirability shot right up from my lower parts to my upper parts and on into the rainy Mexican skies.

Besides her connection with Mingus, she breathed out smug Village hipness, that "I'm a totally cool person" attitude that I, too, needed to manufacture on demand. Whether she was real or just another poser I neither knew nor cared. I wanted every inch of her.

Then I got her. Our affair lasted about a week until a hunky Hollywood screenwriter showed up in his red convertible with his smooth talk and B-movie hunky looks and that was the end of that. I mourned for days.

Meanwhile, Bear had decided not to study painting after all, but instead learn about life through hanging out at La Cucaracha ("The Kook"), drinking *Cuba Libres* and playing dominoes. It seemed like a good plan at the time.

The Kook was an expat bar across the street from the Jardín, a plaza where young men and women strolled the perimeter together on Sunday evenings, ladies clockwise, and gentlemen against their tide. San Miguel's small, but vibrant collection of gringo artists and writers dropped by as time and funds allowed, but the core group who opened and closed the place were there to have a good time, and to drink. They were a friendly bunch, comfortable to be with, getting a little heat on while playing dominoes and perfecting bar tricks. One favorite was a rocket built from match heads and tinfoil that could hopefully launch across the Kook and splash down in Elmer Gustafson's margarita. Another afternoon I watched a guy from Wisconsin pull a 10-peso note from between two beer bottles, one balanced upside down on top of the other, without knocking the bottles over.

Late one April night, or possibly early one April morning – after the Kook closed anyway – Bear took off in the Willys with a few of the regulars. I don't know where they were headed –possibly the old guy with the all-night hot dog cart had gone home early and they wanted something to eat. What I know is Bear took a wrong turn and ended in a cul-de-sac at San Miguel's tiny railroad station (the same place near where Neal Cassady, seven years later, passed out on the tracks and never woke up.) He made a quick U-turn on two wheels and rolled our old burden.

I don't know how he did it. Bear was an ace driver, he must have been blind out of his mind. *La policia* quickly showed up and hauled the carcass off to gringo truck jail. The next day we went to the police station and paid an enormous fine to retrieve its remains. Years later, Bear told me that was when it occurred to him that he and alcohol weren't meant to be friends. If he didn't quit, he was going to end up just another alkie. A few years later, he did quit.

Suddenly we were broke. Bear had the truck running again in a couple of days, but the wheels were hopelessly out of alignment, the right pane of the windshield was in shards and, after ordering a new tire from Celaya down the road, we maybe had enough money for gas to the border.

I didn't care anyway. Without Janice, what did life matter? Let's get out of here.

We couldn't just split though. We had to wait for the stupid tire.

Day after day we sat in the open air cafe across the street from the Jardín, waiting. For a half-dozen evenings, we said good-bye to everybody, then next morning, when the tire still hadn't arrived, said hello again.

Bear and me in the Jardin, San Miguel de Allende, April 1961

Someone heard the U.S. had just invaded Cuba. Castro had supposedly fled to Haiti. No, he had fled to Jamaica. No, he hadn't fled anywhere. Then someone heard that an American in Morelia had his teeth kicked out by a communist mob. Better be careful! Crap, what was going on back home?

We slept where we could, mostly in the truck, until that Hollywood rat who stole Janice invited us to stay at his place. He had an extra bedroom. What a rat, how could I stay mad at him when he insisted on acting like a friend?

We didn't say much as we limped our way north toward Texas. I guess I was still pissed off at Bear for rolling the truck. Or maybe I was just lost in the future, scheming how I could get to New York City for the summer.

I loved San Miguel, I could have stayed on for months, but what the hell – we were on the road again.

Three or four slow days later, we crossed into the Texas border town of Eagle Pass and wired home for funds. When money miraculously arrived the next day, we raced to the first coffee shop we spotted and ordered hamburgers loaded with lettuce and tomato that wouldn't make us sick. We drank chocolate milkshakes. Then we kissed good-bye to our campsite on the Rio Grande, where the mosquitoes sounded like dentist drills and felt like it when they bit us, and checked into the Yellow Rose Motel for a shower and a night in real beds before we hit the road home to the San Mateo. We cracked a couple bottles of Lone Star. It felt sort of good to be back in the States and sort of not.

San Francisco At Last

I'd never heard of Noe Valley. Neither had any of my friends. In fact, in those days, most people weren't sure where Noe Valley was. Somewhere out in the Mission, they supposed. We could probably get close to it by taking the 24 Diviz to the end of the line.

Susan and I did, and we knocked on the door of a nondescript house on 26th Street, at the top of three flights of worn concrete stairs. A frazzled-looking Negro woman answered the door (in 1961, Negro was still the term of respect). Yes, she had a room for rent, it was the attic, did we want to see it? We did, we liked it, and Susan and I rented it.

I was going to share an attic with Susan Haley, my pal Russ's girlfriend. She and Russ were going to get married when they got around to it. Meanwhile, she was going to summer session at San Francisco State and needed a cheap place to live, just like I did.

Susan slept on a mattress at the north end of the attic, I slept on my own mattress at the south end. We didn't know it but we were two flecks on an immigrant stream heading toward the Haight-Ashbury of the Sixties and beyond.

In the summer of 1961, bohemian North Beach had fallen on hard times, but it was still the only cool place to breathe. Noe Valley seemed as far away from North Beach as an aspiring beat poet such as myself could get and still live in San Francisco. Shabby row houses staggered up the streets, old ladies pushed economical shopping carts through the fog to the supermarket on 24th Street for more Rice-A-Roni. Cats yowled in the backyard at night, and that was about it for excitement.

Louise Sterling was the name of the frazzled-looking lady. Her hipster poet husband had run off with a Swedish girl the year before, and left her to lurch through life on her own. She kept up the best front she could, and raised their two kids to be friendly and polite. The residents of a big commune on Fulton Street in the Western Addition had helped to get her boardinghouse up and running.

I had stumbled upon a loose network of communes: the Central Street House, the O'Farrell Street House, the Fulton Street House, and Louise's little outrigger on 26th Street. Later that year, I scored the peyote for my first psychedelic excursion from one of those houses, little green cacti, mailed legally from Rose's Cactus Garden in Laredo.

The Fulton Street People lived in a turreted Queen Anne a couple of blocks west of Divisadero. They shared everything except each other, as far as I knew. They shopped, cooked, cleaned house, and paid the bills communally. Susie and I showed up once or twice a week to take bread with them. I liked the free meals and I got to know people who could teach me stuff.

They were mostly in their mid-20s. They weren't beat. In fact, I couldn't find anyone in the City who admitted to being beat. I learned what I didn't know I knew: people who have found themselves object to being assigned a title of any kind. The Fulton Street people lived together for fun and cheapness and spiritual uplift.

Besides Suzie and me, Louise's place was inhabited by a ragtag collection of stragglers washed up from across America. For instance, Larry from Omaha was a shy little guy with a pencil-line pornographer's mustache, a strapping wife, a nursling baby, and a cleft palate. I rarely understood what he was trying to tell me, but was sure he had valuable information if I could only grab hold of it.

Downstairs lived another of those not-quite-30, dark-haired Jewish artists that haunted my sight in those days, this one from Berkeley. I guess she was resting up for a while in the anonymous back of beyond. She would sit afternoons in our overgrown backyard, sketching with pastels and sipping some kind of mint tea. I thought she might know the meaning of life, but when I asked her, she only whispered something under her breath, then smiled and showed me her sketch. It was just a picture of a sunny backyard in Noe Valley. I didn't get it.

If I'd asked her to explain Pearl to me, she'd probably pet the cat or something. Pearl was a couple of years older than me, had her own apartment on Dolores Street, but materialized at the Fulton Street House from time to time, which is where we met a couple weeks later. A delicate face, guarded blue eyes and fiery red hair worn pixie style, she seemed a kind of changeling girl to me. She lived in a wheelchair from childhood polio, but she could cast magic in the air; I inhaled.

The last thing I needed was another love affair. I was still smarting from losing Janice to that hunky B-movie screenwriter in Mexico. My plan was to wander around the city all day and have someone to play with at night. And Pearl was the most enchanting young woman around.

Once, after we'd been seeing each other for a few weeks, she said I was only interested in her because she'd make a good character in a story. I was flattered at being thought so dedicated to my hypothetical craft, but she misjudged me. I was sincere in all my dealings with beautiful girls.

Wasn't I? Her words got under my skin. What if I wasn't?

I hated that thought. I didn't want to go around all day analyzing my motivation. What's spontaneous about that? And spontaneity was a big deal in my circle. Gypsy Girl used to tell me, "When in doubt, jump and swing."

I was in doubt all right, and after I finished jumping and swinging, there I was – still in doubt. Was I honestly hot for this pixie girl, or was I selfishly exploiting her for story material?

I liked being with Pearl. I liked holding her tight and looking into her mysterious cool eyes and trying to figure out who was in there looking back at me. I just wasn't ready to be serious, see? What's wrong with that? Nothing!

Besides, Pearl's heart was in solitary confinement, who knew what she thought? Maybe she was playing with me. What about that? Why do I always have to be the bad guy?

So, one afternoon I decided to visit some friends from San Miguel. They'd just arrived in the City and rented an apartment on Hyde Street at the edge of the Tenderloin. Dick was a bearded philosopher, older and wiser than me. He lived with a sturdy German girl named Ulla who was easy to talk to while Dick was in his study proving the existence of God on strictly rational grounds.

I figured maybe I could unburden my doubts to Dick and Ulla. They were real beats, people who theoretically understood life, which I certainly didn't. I nervously climbed their apartment building's backstairs.

For a long time I stood outside their back door. It was a kitchen door with a small window, and in the window Dick had taped an index card with this neatly typed message:

"HOUSE OF TRUTH.
NO BULLSHIT PLEASE."

I stood stunned. Fuck. He meant that sign for people like me. Can I speak an authentic word, ever? No, I'm just a bullshitter, pretending to be this big beatnik when inside I'm a trembling kid. I was jiving Pearl so I could get material for my story even though I wasn't writing a story. Saying anything to get what I want. Horrible!

I turned and tiptoed down the stairs. I didn't want Dick and Ulla to know a bullshitter had nearly knocked on their door.

I dragged my feet up Hyde Street, and stopped when I got to Swensen's Ice Cream. I thought some butter brickle would make me feel better, but it didn't. Hands in pockets, staring at the sidewalk, vaguely perceiving clumsy oxfords and hot little heels clomping or clicking past, I climbed to the top of Russian Hill and sat dejected in the twilight on the same balustrade where I had once shouted for joy with Russ and Lazaro, surveying our North Beach empire.

It wasn't my empire any more. I was just another fraud whose self-deception had been exposed. One more phony.

I could never enter the House of Truth until I'd become a true person.

Getting My Ticket Punched, Part II

My newfound determination to become a better person lasted right up until Russ Garibaldi suggested we drive cross-country to New York City in his rebuilt 1950 MG for further adventures and more joy.

No way was I ready to settle down, get my college degree, and, horrors, turn into an English professor with a house in Sea Cliff and a Volvo, my teenage kids having all the fun while I strode around class in a three-piece suit explaining Wallace Stevens. Or, even worse, what if I became a phony Hollywood screenwriter like that rat in San Miguel who stole Janice? What if I ended up living in a ranch burger in Sherman Oaks and churning out episodes of "77 Sunset Strip"?

I had to get to New York right away, city that taught my lost Janice how to be amazing, before it was too late.

Russ and I were full of fundraising ideas. Besides normal free-spirit enterprise like waxing cars and mowing lawns, we invented a hypothetical orphanage in San Miguel de Allende. We drove back to our San Mateo home turf and went door to door collecting cans of food for the poor orphans. Our friends Lazaro and Gypsy Girl worked the other side of the street. It was kicks and pretty soon we had all the beans and fruit cocktail we could fit behind the MG's bucket seats. I bought a saucepan and an oven rack at the Salvation Army, so we were covered there too.

So, before the summer of 1961 had produced any further unhappy love affairs, Russ and I set off across America, Russ's conga strapped to the running board, my guitar's neck sticking out the back pouch of the two-seater, following the great Kerouacian route on U.S. 40 to Denver and on and on across the unknown hinterlands.

The fuel pump crapped out before we got to Sacramento. Russ hitched in to get parts. I lounged under an oak tree, smoking roll-your-owns and guarding our gear. Darkness hit before Russ returned, so we drank coffee and slept under the oaks by the side of the highway and were content.

Next day we skirted Winnemucca in the gloaming.

Witnessed the Great Salt Lake through a rainstorm windshield.

Why did the 770 citizens of Duchesne, Utah, need a dancing school?

We camped up dusty side roads. Once a pickup rattled by and the cowpoke inside solemnly touched his hat in our direction.

Sunup in shirtsleeves.

Brewing cowboy coffee while Russ ran around in his jockstrap shouting hooray.

It *was* kinda thrilling to be out here in the unknown world.

"Good morning, boys," said the cop in Craig, Colorado, without hostility, just saying good morning.

Crossing the Rockies, 11,000 feet high in torrential rain and mist, splattered in construction mud.

The Green Spider, Denver's lonely beatnik outpost.

Farmers grew corn by the mile to feed their pigs. We didn't know it was pig corn, but had we known we wouldn't have cared. It tasted good to us every night. Just a little tough.

Outside Omaha, we sprung an oil leak but had an address. Shy Larry's elderly parents lived downtown in a crumbling third-floor tenement. We knocked on their door and they knew who we were right away. He'd written ahead in case we showed up – what a guy. They fed us all we could eat, potatoes and meat, and gave us sofas to sleep on in the dank summer night.

Next morning, a mechanic said it would cost $120 to fix the leak. Instead, we bought two gallons of heavy oil and kept checking the dipstick as we rolled though Iowa toward the great city of the east.

In Ohio we were caught in a thunderstorm. A farmer let us sleep in his grain silo, along with the millions and millions of insomniac ants he kept imprisoned there. Next morning he told us he didn't know anything about those ants, he'd have to do something, his wife fed us pancakes, we helped him load a truck, then traveled on toward Pennsylvania.

We collected pop bottles along the highway shoulder until we had enough to turn in for their nickel deposits to buy a pound of hamburger. We sopped up the grease with slices of white bread and ate that too.

Full moon over the Alleghenies.

Inhaling carbon monoxide fumes through the Lincoln Tunnel, then the Big Apple.

We found my San Miguel friend Kirk Smallman on East 7th Street. He had a new job, a cameraman for Westinghouse television, so he wasn't around much, but we were welcome to sleep on his floor.

We walked the steamy streets all day. Watched secretaries eating their bag lunches in Bryant Park. We drank beer at McSorley's Old Ale House. Took the night ferry to Staten Island and stood on deck in the rain. Ate in a cheap dairy restaurant on Second Avenue. Learned of the existence of knishes, blintzes, pirogies, kasha, borscht, and matzo ball soup, and I ordered more the next day. Dragged Russ to the Radio City Music Hall to see the Rockettes but mostly to see the new film *Fanny* starring Leslie Caron. Because, in spite of being totally hip, I was in love with her. At the White Horse Tavern we paid homage to the bar stool where Dylan Thomas drunk himself to death eight years before.

We went Gerde's Folk City to see a folksinger Kirk told us about, Bob Dylan, but Peter Yarrow was topping the bill that night. We never heard of him. If you're under 30, you've probably never heard of him either, but he was big for a while with Peter, Paul and Mary. Later he used to come around the Haight a lot. I'd see him in the Panhandle, sitting on a log with his girlfriend listening to the Grateful Dead, acting like a normal person. He couldn't fool me. He was Peter Yarrow. I saw him at Folk City in 1961.

I met a girl who worked for Grosset & Dunlap, publisher of the Nancy Drew books. So far her career consisted of answering letters from 11-year-olds to Carolyn Keene, Nancy's fictitious author. Jodie was a minion, but an employed minion working for a real publisher, and for work she impersonated a famous imaginary author. I was so impressed I got too wasted to walk back to Kirk's apartment and slept the night in her bathtub, because I'd still never met a girl who would have sex on her first date. They might be out there, though, and I was hoping to find out.

We stayed on East 7th Street most of the summer. I thought I'd already seen it all, except I'd never seen a cockroach before. Or a police lock with an iron bar, one end bolted to the front door and the other end jammed in a floor slot to keep junkie burglars out. I'd seen a few jingle-jangle mornings, though.

Our time in Manhattan wore on and eventually our welcome wore out. Besides, we had to get home in time for the fall semester at San Francisco State, the big time at last!

We crossed the Bay Bridge at four o'clock in the morning into golden Frisco with our hipness tickets punched. Within weeks, I would eat peyote and see God.

Solveig Hitches Home

I

I have no artifacts from that phase of my life when Solveig tried to shut her lights forever. Or of the night I tore a gash in my hand so deep I can see it still, 50 years later, its pale scar like a fountain pen nib driving deep into my palm. I have no photographs, no ban-the-bomb leaflets, no empty bottles of codeine cough syrup, no filthy ashtrays, no breaking hearts beating in rhythm, only my fine-haired memory of her brave little face.

Solveig and I were friends, that's all. I was through with love. I'd already tried it with a 17-year-old with auburn hair and braces on her teeth named Carmen O'Shaughnessy, and it hadn't worked out. She coaxed me and teased me until I gave her a key I didn't know I had, then she twisted it shut and it hurt.

But Solveig and I could sit in peace at the bleak kitchen table of our student flat at Eighth and Judah in wintry 1961 San Francisco – in the time of the bombs – and drink instant coffee and consider the mysteries of our blind hearts and lost childhoods. Nobody was trying to get over on anybody.

On the weekends, we'd sometimes walk together in Golden Gate Park. At 19, she'd already seen a lot, although she hadn't learned anything yet, and I liked to listen to her. I liked to feel her honeyed European accent flowing through me. One day, somewhere along the edge of Stow Lake, she told me her convoluted story and here's how it went:

She'd been born and raised in Spain under the regime of Generalissimo Franco, when the sight of his *Guardia Civil*

67

coming down the street in their green uniforms, black hats, their submachine guns, meant lower your eyes and don't speak. They might claim they heard you say something offensive, and then your parents might never see you again.

Her parents were Latvian. Back in the Thirties, her journalist father had been sent to Spain to cover the raging civil war, and he found he could gather the news quite safely by sitting in a bar in Bilbao and chatting with the soldiers who came in. He got to like Bilbao, and after the civil war ended, sent for his fiancée. Franco's dictatorship must have looked pretty good compared with the Nazi armies massed to the west of his homeland and Soviet armies poised to invade from the east.

Her father wasn't interested in politics. Solveig called him an opportunist, and Franco's Spain was his opportunity. He and his young bride Izabella built a life in Bilbao, on the north coast of the Basque Country. He opened a photography studio and did well. Solveig and her brothers and sister were born there.

The family had a cook, someone to clean, a nanny and a woman who came to iron their clothes. One of their maids took Solveig home with her in the summers to live in a medieval village and play on the mountain slopes. To me, San Francisco born and raised, she seemed to have stepped from some profound black and white foreign film like *Forbidden Games*.

Solveig in the Pyrenees, 1948. (photo: Rochanah Weissinger)

When Solveig was 15 her father lost his money. She didn't know why, or how it happened, but eventually someone offered him a job in Florida. They sold everything they had to pay for their tickets and a car once they reached the States. And in November 1957, they emigrated.

Solveig arrived in Florida speaking no English. At night, her father taught her what little he knew, and she learned rapidly, but spoke with a never-before-heard Latvian/Castilian accent. Later, a speech professor told her that for the first time in his career he was "befuddled" because he couldn't pinpoint a student's accent.

Life in Florida was not quite what they had hoped. Except for her father, their English was nonexistent, they had no support system, and the employment her father had been promised evaporated. Her upper-middle-class mother had to take a job cleaning hotel rooms, her businessman father worked in the hotel kitchen, Solveig and her sister were sent to be "mother's helpers" in Miami.

I think this is when Solveig's tough nature first showed itself – in how quickly she adapted to her new life, how she set herself to learn English, and how she was able to view her family's descent into chaos as an adventure. For her parents, it wasn't so easy. Her father began drinking, and her mother tumbled into a black depression.

In the spring of 1958, her father finally found a real job, and they moved to Fort Lauderdale. Barely 16 but capable in spite of her elementary English, Solveig snagged work making malted milkshakes, sandwiches and hamburgers at a drugstore downtown.

By fall she thought she had enough English to finish high school, and she registered at Pompano Beach High. She told them she was 17 so they would admit her as a senior. Her senior year was a blur, she said, she could remember nothing of it. I figured I knew why: she'd never heard of Buddy Holly. She'd never driven down the midnight streets of Pompano Beach in her boyfriend's '56 Chevy. Instead, she was in her room reading Sartre's *Roads to Freedom* and Camus' *The Stranger* in Spanish for desire of something I wanted too. She rode to school on the Vespa she bought with her summer savings, which immediately marked her as a hopeless European intellectual, a weirdo, a square from nowhere.

I knew all about Buddy Holly and I had danced the bop in my desert boots at the sock hop, but I wanted it too, whatever it was. In high school daydreams, I rode across France on my Vespa with a beautiful Spanish-Latvian girl on the back holding a baguette and a bottle of wine for our picnic by the glimmering sea, except I hadn't met any girls like that yet. I wanted to be with artists and poets and revolutionaries, people who thought about things that mattered. I wanted to be a Dharma Bum, and I wanted to love someone for real. I wanted to be free, really free. And we both wanted something else too, something better than any of that. But neither of us knew what it was or where we might find it. It wasn't in our flat on Judah Street.

In spite of her ignorance of high school social skills, the school awarded her a four-year scholarship to Florida State with all expenses paid – tuition, books, room and board. She was astonished. She hadn't even understood what a graduation ceremony was, so she didn't bother to go. After her triumph, her parents rented a cap and gown and had graduation pictures taken at a studio.

Solveig at 17 (photo: Rochanah Weissinger)

Her mother was renewed, filled with ambition for her brilliant daughter. She knew they could never afford to send Solveig to college on their own.

In early September 1959, her parents drove her the 450 miles upstate to Tallahassee. They packed everything the school said she needed into two suitcases – clothes, sheets, towels, and her English dictionary. None of the three had ever been to a college before. They didn't know what to expect.

There weren't many other kids there yet. James Rimkeit carried his daughter's bags up three flights of stairs to her room. A bunk bed, a desk, a chair, four bare walls, a small window that opened onto a fire escape. To Solveig, it looked a jail cell.

She wanted to go home, but when she saw her mother's bewildered face, more frightened than her own, she smiled and looked confident.

Izabella said, "I'll send curtains."

Solveig hugged her mother one last time, then they drove away. She threw herself on the bare mattress and cried for an hour. She'd never been alone like this before, over 400 miles from home. She had almost no money, she didn't know how to work the pay phone in the lobby, and she didn't know how to make a collect call home.

II

The Solveig I knew in January 1962, the one sitting beside me on the crackled green bench beside Stow Lake, was sleeping with two guys, both friends of mine. She was sure she must be in love with both of them and was trying to decide which one she loved best, but somehow didn't seem to be in love with either of them and couldn't understand why, or even if, and it was driving her crazy. She was seeing a psychologist on campus at the Student Health Center, but so far he wasn't helping.

I usually listened to her with pale self-absorbed attention. She sounded like absinthe to me, far away, sweet as syrup, wrapping around my own ache inside. She had never told me all this stuff before, and for once I was paying attention.

III

Solveig didn't stay down long. She snuffled and dried her eyes and went downstairs for dinner. This wasn't the first time she'd been pushed into the world – she remembered those first months in America when she'd cared for strangers' babies in Miami Beach. She'd cried those nights away too. But then her father had come to take her home on Friday evenings. She knew this time there would be no going home. She would never truly go home again.

She started out the semester well – she was attractive, she made friends easily, she made straight A's easily too. She didn't really fit into Florida State's party school culture, but she *did* fit in with the other outsiders on campus – the "fringe element." The dean of women noticed right away.

The Philosophy Club, Spring 1960 (Photo: Rochanah Weissinger)

Solveig and her new circle of friends soon started an on-campus group called the Philosophy Club. They purportedly met to discuss existentialism or Aristotle or something, but soon they were discussing the incipient civil rights movement, and how they could get involved in it.

FSU was segregated, of course. There was a college in Tallahassee for Negroes too, but white students weren't allowed on campus there without written permission from their parents. Growing up in the Basque country, Solveig had seen prejudice against the Basque people – they weren't allowed to speak their native language in public – but never racism. She thought it was ridiculous, absurd.

The Philosophy Club decided to attend a CORE (Congress of Racial Equality) meeting at A&M, the nearby Negro school. None of them owned a car, so they hiked across town and, when they arrived on campus, conveniently forgetting they needed their parents' permission to be there, Solveig asked a student where the meeting was. He mumbled something unintelligible and sped away. Maybe he thought white students on campus meant trouble, and he didn't want to be around for it.

If so, he was right. They were still looking for the meeting when two prowl cars rolled up, lights flashing. The cops jumped out, pushed the girls into the back of one car, the guys into the other, and off they raced.

"They were furious, I thought they were taking us to jail." Solveig told me, "They called me a communist, a pinko whore. They called me a nigger-loving cunt. The spit from their mouths splattered all over me. I was so scared, I peed on myself."

She knew next to nothing about U.S. law, but in Spain, if the *Guardia Civil* pulled you in for a political offense, you could be tortured, raped, or even killed.

However, after harassing them for half an hour, the cops dumped the girls somewhere in the ghetto, "where your nigger friends can help you." They walked aimlessly until an empty cab rolled by. Back on campus, they learned the same thing had happened to the men in the other car.

By the next day, Solveig was branded on campus as a niggerlover, an outside agitator, and probably a communist. This was not a good reputation for a scholarship student, even if she *was* barely 17. The dean of woman made another note in her file.

IV

It was Christmas vacation, 1961, or maybe it was semester break, I don't remember. Only a few of the People, as we called ourselves (meaning the people who mattered), stayed in town, so Solveig and I spent long hours together. If we didn't sit in our kitchen and talk, we caught the streetcar to the beach and walked along the water's edge and talked. Or, like today, we wandered around Golden Gate Park.

Mostly we pondered her life, where she was going, what the shrink at school had said, and sometimes we pondered my life and why was I so unhappy inside and why did I crave Carmen so bad when it was clear she was just fooling around with me?

V

In the late winter of 1959, Solveig met a student from Key West named Roland Andros, who lived off campus. They started going out together. One evening, Solveig and Roland were sitting on his ratty sofa, watching "Route 66" and making out. They fell asleep in each other's arms. When Solveig woke, she realized she had missed lockout.

In those days, college dorms were segregated by sex. Among their responsibilities, administrators were expected to make sure their female students remained virgins. Curfews were part of their armory. I could take a dorm girl out for coffee, should I ever want to, but she had to be back inside before lockout. Freshmen girls had it the worst. Curfew on a weeknight came as early as 9:30 p.m. Miss it and you were grounded.

Solveig dashed the few blocks to the dorm. She knew if she rang the doorbell, she'd be grounded for sure. She also remembered her window was unlocked. If she climbed the fire escape, maybe she could get inside without anybody noticing.

It worked. Even her friendly roommate was down-stairs. She slipped on her nightgown and joined her fellow students brushing their teeth in the bathroom. Right away, she knew something was wrong – the room went quiet, no one would even look at her. Someone, maybe with a grudge against rule-breaking outsiders with foreign accents, had ratted on her.

Next morning she was ordered to the dean of women's office. The dean didn't invite her to sit down. She gave Solveig a baleful look and told her she was expelled right now. Maybe she was relieved to get rid of a potential troublemaker so easily. Solveig already had a reputation on campus. Now, she had not only broken curfew, but she had lied about it by sneaking up the fire escape.

The dean gave Solveig 24 hours to get off campus. She walked, trembling, through the unclouded streets of Tallahassee to Roland's apartment and told him what had happened. Roland was outraged. An hour later he stormed into the dean of men's office and quit school on the spot.

The next morning, they caught the Greyhound together for Pompano Beach. Solveig had to tell her mother that hopes for her brilliant daughter would have to wait.

The meeting went okay, but the next morning her mother stayed in bed. She hadn't slept. She had a headache. Something hurt.

VI

From Pompano Beach, Solveig and Roland took the bus to Key West to tell his parents what had happened. After they navigated through that difficult scene, they went to the beach, ate key lime pie, and decided to go to Boston, where Roland had friends at MIT. They were a couple now.

She told me she and Roland were never in love, had never had sex, never spent the night together, didn't really know each other. Yet here they were, pushed into the world by a foolish action, an unjust consequence, and a courageous but rash gesture.

VII

They climbed off the bus into snow-covered Boston with no money, no mittens, no hats, no love, and looked up Roland's pals. After a few days there, they rented a basement apartment on credit in the student neighborhood near Harvard Square. Solveig found a job making change at a cafeteria. Roland unloaded trucks. They started sleeping together.

Joan Baez was playing the Club 47, down the street from their apartment. She'd been a smash at the Newport Folk Festival the preceding fall, and now crowds waiting to get in the club straggled past their apartment house. Solveig and Roland watched them, sometimes they heard her voice out the club's door for a moment, but they strolled on. They were saving for next fall's tuition at Florida State. They intended to go back on their own terms.

Evenings, they sat in a Harvard Square coffee shop surrounded by the blazing student intelligentsia. Sometimes they joined conversations about integration or Joan Baez or Jack Kerouac or nuclear disarmament or oral contraception or François Truffaut or LSD. Sometimes they just sat quietly, not speaking to each other, watching the intelligentsia lighting their low-tar, filter-tipped, mentholated cigarettes.

Solveig didn't light up. Maybe she ordered an English muffin with orange marmalade. Maybe as the night drew on, she rubbed the brown ring of cream scum from her coffee cup.

In April 1960, Solveig's mother decided to visit. She wanted to find out what was going on up there, and Solveig thought, "She'll see we're living together! She'll find out we're having sex!"

Roland, with that reckless code of honor he'd displayed in Tallahassee, suggested they go to City Hall and get married. That seemed like a simple solution, so they did. They paid their fee, signed the papers, came back the next day, stood in line at the city clerk's office, and then they were married. They celebrated their wedding dinner at the cafeteria where Solveig worked.

VIII

Not quite two years later in San Francisco, we finished circumnavigating Stow Lake and crossed the footbridge onto the island in the center called Strawberry Hill. There's a view from the hilltop – we could see the sun-washed towers of St. Ignatius in the near distance, and the Russ Building downtown. Beyond them, the hills of the East Bay were starting to turn green from winter rain, and beyond lay vast America.

I was gazing at that view, but I didn't see it. It was obstructed by this Spaniard, this Latvian, this whoever, whatever she was beside me, my Solveig, her fine wheaten hair trembling in the breeze, her black-rimmed pointy glasses slipping down her nose. Some kind of tendrils were sprouting from inside me to wrap around her forever.

But I didn't understand any of that yet. I just was happy to be with her, and I wanted to know more of what happened when they got back to Tallahassee.

She said it was a different city than the one they had left in February. While they'd been in Boston, a group of Negro college students had staged one of the first sit-ins in the South at a Woolworth's lunch counter. They were refused service, arrested, hauled to jail, and served their sentence. But as soon as they were released, they set up picket lines around the segregated department stores, and more students, some white, joined them. By the time Solveig and Roland blew back into town, white Tallahassee was fed up and pissed off.

Solveig and Roland found a house a few blocks from campus and invited four of Roland's Key West pals to share the rent. They bought used mattresses and furniture from the Salvation Army. Roland's friends added some travel posters, a study lamp, books, and a dark-haired girl with a pixie cut named Shelly.

The guys, except, theoretically, Roland, were mad for Shelly, and she liked them. She particularly liked ruling over them, and they were okay with that – if it meant a chance to get into bed with her. Shelly installed herself in the second bedroom, while the men slept in the living room. Each in turn spent three nights in Shelly's bedroom, going round and round in a fair and equitable rotation. Solveig lay awake and listened to orgasms battering the thin walls from the next room. What were they doing in there? What was she missing? She'd never even *had* an orgasm. (Of course, she didn't tell me that part until long after.)

Shelly had everything and Solveig had nothing. That's how she felt. No one was madly in love with Solveig, certainly not Roland. At least Roland wasn't sniffing after Shelly too. She was pretty sure he wasn't.

The house quickly became a meeting place for white students who supported the sit-ins. Solveig admitted to me she hadn't understood the social issues or politics, she just knew the way Negroes in Tallahassee were treated disgusted her. She had never studied U.S. history. She had no thought-out philosophy. To her, the conflict was idealistic youth pitted against, as she put it with her own light touch of discrimination, "fat, ignorant Southern men."

A scholarship student named Jefferson Poland moved in, the only white member on the board of Tallahassee's CORE office and, at 19, already well known to the police: a troublemaker. He'd been arrested in the Woolworth's sit-in and served his time.

One morning they woke to find a sign that said "Niggerlovers Live Here" punched into their front lawn. Sometimes nightriders dumped cans of garbage on their front lawn, or heaved empty beer bottles against the house. One night, a brick crashed through their living room window. Another night, they saw dark figures on the lawn, then a BB gun shot pierced their newly replaced window. After that, when they heard the squeal of tires flying around the corner late at night, and a pickup truck gunning its engine, they hit the floor fast. Solveig was sure the rednecks were going to burn the house down. Maybe they would die in there.

They were also afraid of going to jail. Jefferson told them stories about what had happened to him in there. They had no money for bail. So, when the spring semester ended, the housemates decided as a group they were going to move to San Francisco. They didn't know anyone there, but San Francisco was supposed to be the center of freedom and coolness. But Solveig didn't go with them at first. She decided to go home for the summer to earn some money.

IX

It was September before Solveig, now 19, arrived in San Francisco and knocked on the door of Roland's boarding-house in the Haight-Ashbury. A stranger answered. Yes, Roland lived there, but they hadn't seen him in days. No, she couldn't stay there that night; the owners didn't want strangers crashing. Well, okay, you can sleep here for a couple nights, but you need to hide your sleeping bag, so they'll think you're just hanging out...

After two days of waiting, she knew Roland was avoiding her. When she finally managed to track him down, she found him with a new motorcycle and a lanky redhead to go with it. She got the picture.

Solveig walked away, through the Panhandle of Golden Gate Park under the ancient eucalyptus trees. The afternoon fog wisped through her hair. She sat on a bench outside the playground and watched the young mothers in poplin coats pushing their baby strollers. She wrapped herself in her arms. The fog thickened. If she was going to live in San Francisco, she'd have to get a coat.

Damn it, she really didn't like him that much either.

X

One bright October morning about a month following her debacle with Roland, I heard Solveig's honeyed voice for the first time. I was loitering in front of the Student Peace Union's table outside the San Francisco State Commons, and she was talking to the student behind the table about American missile bases in Turkey. I didn't know there were any, but I knew I liked that voice, so I struck up a conversation. She was living in a boarding-house across the street from the Panhandle, washing dishes in exchange for rent, but she didn't like it. I told there was going to be a room coming open where I lived. With six to eight students sharing each flat, the rent was cheap to nonexistent, and since we were all part of the peace movement, we had a common bond. Maybe she'd like that better? Then we progressed to the radioactive subject of the moment: the Bomb.

It wasn't an academic issue. Whenever I opened the kitchen window, I could smell the world coming to an end out there. I could see the sky turning blood red. In my dreams I heard Russian bombers roaring over the Golden Gate Bridge.

Only a few days before, the Russians had dropped a 50-megaton hydrogen bomb on their Arctic island, Novaya Zemlya. Still the largest bomb ever exploded, it could have vaporized San Francisco in a couple of seconds, with room left over to atomize Mill Valley, Berkeley and San Mateo too. The Soviets could blast American cities into oblivion whenever Nikita Khrushchev got mad enough. And he wasn't acting like a really stable guy.

John Kennedy advised Americans to start building fallout shelters.

A few days after I met Solveig, a girl named Belladonna DeNapoli invited me to a candlelit dinner at her sexy apartment on Masonic Avenue. When I arrived, I learned Bella's grandmother had suddenly broken her fibula or something, Bella had flown to the hospital to be by her side, and I was greeted instead by her preternaturally beautiful roommate, 17-year-old Carmen O'Shaughnessy from the desert lands beyond Palm Springs.

I brought my guitar, of course. I never went anywhere without it. I sang "Goin' down to the river, gonna take my rockin' chair" while she stirred my stew, and she sang "I met her in Venezuela with a basket on her head" while she spread honey on my biscuits, and after dinner she pulled off her dress and ran naked down the creaking stairs into the rainy backyard and danced like a hare in the pink cloudlight. I stood on the porch in my dirty wool chaleco and Buddy Holly glasses and ratty beat huaraches in dumbfounded awestruck wonder.

XI

Carmen and I took to each other right away. Maybe we fell in love with our visions of who we might be later, if we didn't chicken out. She liked to portray herself as an untamed wild child, and I was convinced that's exactly who she was. Some days she'd come to school wearing tight Levi's, high-top logger boots, and a green-checked mackinaw like she'd just come off the winter desert. When the weather was warm she wore a Guatemalan peasant skirt, an embroidered blouse, and handmade sandals with long straps wrapping around her calves. She wore her tawny hair flying free, or in long braids whipping behind her. When we were alone, she wore, best of all, nothing at all. Each look was a marker, an arrow shot toward the place we were both trying to get to.

Illuminated by the light of Carmen's cat-green eyes, I found new ways to portray beatness, what it looked like to be cut loose from the chains of the skyway, as Bob Dylan put it. Each day I forged a new street dog reality. I became a psychedelic wanderer, a folksinging vagabond, Lord Byron in rags. We taught each other dances with no steps, and thrilled in each other's perfect presence.

There was a burning intensity in Carmen I could never quite match. Like one night in Foster's Cafeteria, we held a staring match. She liked to play that game. Eyes locked, straight-faced, staring to win, and I blinked first. If I hadn't, we might still be there.

Once, we were with friends driving down the Great Highway along San Francisco's ocean coast in the midst of a driving rainstorm. The wind rocked the car, waves crashed against the seawall, and we crept along until Carmen cried she had to get out right now, she'd die if she didn't get out, so we pulled to the side of the road. She leapt into the wind, she danced with it, fell back against it in delight, and the wind held her in a kind of stormy orgasm. Afterward, she climbed back in the car with the rest of us, quiet, wet, spent, happy. Solveig looked across the seat at me and rolled her eyes. She didn't much like Carmen. Girls rarely did.

But for me she was a dream come true. I hate to say that, it's a cliché I know, but there it is, she was my dream come true. In her presence I felt bigger than I ever had before. I wonder if she ever felt that way about me; it would have been perfect.

XII

On Halloween night, October 1961, the Student Peace Union held an all-night vigil on campus to protest the resumption of hydrogen bomb explosions in the Soviet Union and its threatened reappearance in the deserts of Nevada. I played my guitar and sang through the night, sang every sad or funny or angry song I knew, over and over, "House of the

Rising Sun" and "The Great Silkie" and "Pretty pretty pretty Peggy Sue" and "Black girl, black girl, don't you lie to me" and "Just like a tree that's standing by the water, we shall not be moved" and "There once was a union maid who never was afraid" and "You cheated, you lied, you said that you loved me."

Solveig huddled in her sleeping bag as the fog came down, frat rats launched eggs at us and Eva Bessie got egg yolk in her hair, Tess Faraday cried and Mike Skinner made a speech and Floyd Salas made another speech and Don Le Claire smiled beatifically at all without prejudice and flirted with Carmen while the student police cruised by in their little clown car. When cold dawn came, the Commons opened and we drank coffee and blinked at each other as seagulls shrieked high but no birds sang.

In November, the Nevada desert was shaken by hidden underground atomic tests. Clouds of strontium-90 and mists of iodine-131 were released into the air and soon detected floating over Salt Lake City, then found in mothers' milk, then in babies' teeth. Radioactive chemicals had been blowing through the deserts of the West throughout the 1950s but I didn't know anything about it then because in high school I had been focused on learning to play "Peggy Sue" and rolling up my short-sleeved shirt sleeves exactly one-half inch, finding a way to fit in to my high school world and still be me, yelling *Bearcats Bash Burlingame Tonight!* Because why not? As the clouds drifted above us, we cruised the Bayshore freeway, oblivious in our uncertainty.

XIII

In December, the Student Peace Union, meaning us, decided to take action against this pathological arms race, but this being 1961, the only action we could think of was to go somewhere and march around holding signs. We decided the White House would be a likely place. We found a young guy from Berkeley who wanted to join us, and his professor father loaned him the family microbus for the trip. His name was Patrick. As soon as Christmas vacation began, Solveig, Carmen, myself and as many peaceniks as could fit in a VW microbus hit the road.

We planned to cut across the USA and back again in two weeks, driving 24 hours a day, stopping only for food, gas and bathroom breaks. We were going to stay with Solveig's family once we got there – her father had found a new job driving for one of the embassies. For two or three days we would picket the White House, then head for home.

Patrick took the southern route to avoid snow. I sat on my sleeping bag roll and watched the San Joaquin Valley unwind in December grays and browns. I sang a few Pete Seeger songs and made out with Carmen. I watched the sere fields and then the desert swim by. I huddled with Solveig. I tried to sleep.

A young couple had heard about our expedition and joined us just before we left. They were grad students, a little older and better dressed. The husband wore a bohemian style goatee, but beneath it he was an earnest, idealistic above-ground type, possibly a Quaker, who came at Ban the Bomb from a thought-out perspective. I couldn't talk with them about unilateral versus multilateral disarmament. I didn't even know the name of the secretary of defense. I was coming squarely out of fear, anger, rage at the world for putting everything I could ever know or love on the line for the sake of power-jostling on the world's dim stage. I didn't know anything about the military-industrial complex; I wasn't literate on the subject. But I knew somewhere out there Kennedy and Khrushchev were playing an astral game of missile-gap poker and, to them, we meant less than the green felt on the poker table.

Shortly after dawn of our second morning on the road, Patrick rolled the microbus on a patch of ice. He'd been behind the wheel since Berkeley. The rollover broke a window on one side, knocked the wheels out of alignment. There were dents everywhere and the passenger door

85

opened with a horrible creaking sound. My guitar was smashed, the right lens of my glasses broken. I taped a piece of cardboard where the glass had been. We righted the bus, dropped the Quaker couple at the Greyhound station (they had already had quite enough), and traveled on toward the eastern light, stopping for coffee, ordering whatever was cheapest on the menu, laughing, screaming, then staring out the window into the snow that wasn't supposed to be there. I watched Desolation Mesa slide by far on the horizon.

We stopped at the Conoco station, the Sunoco station, the Crazy Eddie station, the America First station, the Stinking Men's Room station and the Mr. Peanut Bar station through Christian Anti-Communist Texas, then fat belted, silver-buckled Oklahoma where the snow came down again as I watched lonely Midwestern two-lane landscapes drift by and a palomino watching us pass by from the door of his red barn by the gunmetal silo. We ate oatmeal with cream and sugar in a Missouri coffee shop while convivial farmers ignored us at dawn.

I tried to get Carmen's jeans off under her shredded Mexican blanket on the vibrating floor over the ravening highways of pre-interstate America. I couldn't get enough of her, but I couldn't get very much of her. I watched her show Peter Weissinger how to eat the white out of an orange peel. He had his hand on her thigh. I played kissy-face with Solveig to show Carmen I didn't care, except I did. I liked Solveig, but I loved Carmen. Wasn't this desperate pain I felt when she ignored me called love?

The black Ohio reflected a sorrowful moon as we passed by the Dickensian warehouses of Cincinnati at midnight. By now we were taking turns driving, and the miles were covered with no more disasters, just plenty of dexies.

XIV

We pulled into Hyattsville, a suburb on the outskirts of Washington, on Monday morning. Solveig's father was at work, her brothers in school. Her lovely, noncontroversial older sister Mirabella met us at the door, and Solveig's long-suffering mother stood behind her. What could she have thought, poor immigrant? I, in particular, looked like a crazy beggar with my unkempt beard and lopsided glasses with missing lens and suffering 19-year-old heart. Yet I didn't feel unwelcome. Perhaps I wasn't feeling much of anything besides the lack of Carmen. Together they found places for us to lay down our sleeping bags, the men on the living room floor, the women in Mirabella's room.

We spent the afternoon shopping for art cards and marker pens, then drew picket signs on their kitchen table. We had already decided to demonstrate our commitment by fasting for 48 hours. It probably wouldn't be long enough to stop atmospheric testing, but it sounded like a stretch to us.

WE ARE FASTING FOR PEACE

WE ARE FASTING TO DEFEND LIFE

BAN THE BOMB!

STUDENT PEACE UNION -- SAN FRANCISCO

with the peace symbol hand drawn at the bottom of each sign. We still called it the Aldermaston symbol, after the English peace march where it was first used.

As I outlined the letters, I wondered about Solveig's father, his history. The Cold War was in full swing, and he was an immigrant from behind the Iron Curtain. I'd never heard of such a thing before. They had moved to Hyattsville from Florida after he conveniently found a job driving a limo for the German Embassy. Was he an agent or counter-agent? Was he CIA? A soldier in some right-wing conspiracy? Or was he what he appeared to be, a poor slob who drank more than was good for him, and hoped he wouldn't be investigated just because he let freethinking bearded beatnik anti-bomb pinko agitators stay in his house.

But he let us stay anyway. We were his daughter's friends. Who he really was, I would never know.

The next morning we found our way through the streets of Washington to the White House. Nobody bothered us. The Park Police were polite. No, we didn't need a permit, just don't chain ourselves to the White House gate. The only other picketer was a man who wanted to bring back Prohibition. We walked in a circle around and around for two days singing "We Shall Overcome" and "Which Side Are You On?" and "Kumbaya," and I wished my guitar wasn't lying in pieces in a snowdrift. Solveig and I grinned at each other from time to time across the picket line. We had brought leaflets to hand out to passersby but no one passed by. In fact, people went out of their way to avoid us, except for occasionally hurling rude remarks from across the street. The security guards ignored us. Finally, we ignored ourselves.

Why, in the face of the world's blind indifference, did we continue? Well, for one thing, I was on an adventure with the people I cared most about in the world. We were together, shouting into the wind of the world's indifference, and it felt good. We were away from home, away from everything we knew, and we were protesting against the devastation before it actually happened. Besides, I was still pretending Carmen wanted to be my girl. I didn't notice any resemblance to Top 40 sentiment.

I was under a spell that crept from somewhere inside me. One night I walked through the leafless Hyattsville neighborhood streets alone – screaming inside, bleeding mental tears, and slugging every impotent telephone pole I passed. Carmen had done something again with someone, I don't remember what.

Solveig had her own reasons, but we never talked about them. I knew she had a finely honed sense of justice and I knew she was revolted by the arrogance currently masquerading as the arms race. But I also knew she wanted to see her mother, and we were staying with Mom. I knew she felt like she was drifting to a dead end in her heart. And she didn't know how to climb into a meaningful life. And, of course, she was 19. It wasn't our fault we were young.

Our 48 hours were done and gone. We splurged on burgers and shakes at a fast food drive-up, and when we got back to Hyattsville, Solveig's Mom had made spaghetti. We ate that too. We slept on their living room floor one more night, then we set out for San Francisco.

The gloomy highway under white snow-filled skies rolled west. Outside Council Bluffs, we picked up a hitchhiker named Carl Gorski. In spite of his commie-sounding name, he was as American as an atom bomb. He was a creative writing major at the university, off on his adventures, Jack Kerouacing across the country alone for kicks and more joy like it said in Jack's book. We hit it off right away and he traveled to San Francisco with us. Solveig liked him a lot. Carl liked Solveig too. They got together.

At a truck stop in the Mojave, Carmen swung off the bus and hitched a ride home across the desert. The last I saw of her that year she was wearing my Mexican chaleco and her high-top logger boots and her lion tawny hair in two long braids, and there was nothing I could do. It was her life and she had a right to get herself raped and killed if she wanted to, she knew what she was doing, she was 17 and strong in spirit. And later I found out that trucker had done her no harm and dropped her outside her desert hometown and she walked the rest of her way home whistling. For who could ever harm Carmen O'Shaughnessy?

XV

Back in San Francisco, I went home for a few days, but home was a foreign land now. I saw my old friends from high school, but there was a gulf between us. I caught the Greyhound back to San Francisco, back to the house on Judah Street. I wanted to see Carmen, but that was impossible. At least I would be with Solveig, but she was wrapped in her new love affair. Instead, I spent the evenings in the front room with the People. We told stories and listened to Miles Davis and Joan Baez.

We invented a parlor game. We would put on a record at random. It had to be something long, because it was going to be the sound track of a movie we improvised as we went along. The first player had to set the scene and start the plot rolling, then anyone could shout out bits of action and dialogue based on the changes in the music. Of course, the real object was to make everyone laugh. Laughter was cheap, and there was no marijuana to be had that we knew about. Besides, at $20 a lid, it might as well have been fine cognac. Maybe we could have pooled our funds and bought a joint. We drank Val-Vin Burgundy, $1.29 a gallon from the corner grocery. Once, we tried pouring lighter fluid on a handkerchief and inhaling it to see what might happen. It made us laugh harder.

Christmas vacation dragged on. Carmen returned. We all decided to go camping together at McClure's Beach on the far northern coast of Point Reyes. Don LeClaire knew how to make mussel stew so we brought along the ingredients, except for mussels, which we scraped off rocks in the surf while the tide was out. We gathered driftwood for the fire, someone broke open the gallon of Val-Vin, Carmen attempted Bisquick biscuits on the coals with a degree of success...and a degree of failure. We ate them anyway. My guitar still lay in splinters in that snowbank, so we brought Don's Mexican nylon string and I sang into the red sunset as the starry night came down.

Clear and cold January night on the roaring beach. Joe Lang, a black-rimmed intellectual from Sacramento who was Solveig's other sometime lover, myself and Solveig walked together far down the beach. Joe gave Solveig his red-checked mackinaw because she was shivering. We watched the luminescent breakers crashing offshore, for miles it seemed, like we were transported to another, more beautiful and stranger planet. As we scuffed the damp sand by the edge of the sea, bright glittering creatures leaped up and scattered like sparks of pixie dust. I showed Solveig and Joe how to link arms and skip like Dorothy and the Tin Woodman and the Scarecrow, and sing "We're Off to See the Wizard" in random notes together as sparks of scudded sand light flew up to our knees.

Friends forever. I knew one thing: we would be friends forever.

When we returned to the fire, Peter Weissinger was noodling on his harmonica. Carmen was curled up beside Don LeClaire. He poked a stick into the fire and it flared. We watched it burn higher. I knew it was over.

At least they didn't zip their sleeping bags together.

In the gray dawn, Don built up the fire to boil water for cowboy coffee, we hauled our gear up the cliff and drove miles along a rutted ranch road that led to the foggy highway that led to suburban Marin County and the Golden Gate Bridge and then the house on Judah Street.

XVI

My life began to fall apart. Like my grades, for instance. I guess I'd forgotten the part about going to class and writing term papers. And I was having trouble with that damn glass wall sliding down between me and the rest of the world. I never knew when it was going to happen. I could hear my friends and see them, but I was powerless to speak. I would have to sit in the kitchen or on somebody's mattress with a beatific smile on my face until it lifted. It was okay, it was nice and safe in there but...what the hell? It wasn't normal. Then it would slide up again and I'd be back aching for Carmen, and feeling my nerves on fire. It was sliding down more often.

I thought maybe the peyote had something to do with it. On my second visit to peyote land, back in September, I had sunk into an area of my mind I hadn't known existed, down through my dreams and memories, until I came to a bright ocean, bright like I was looking directly into an illuminated light bulb from inches away. I'd come out at the bottom of my mind, and it was like that ocean in *Journey to the Center of the Earth* where Pat Boone has to fight the dinosaurs. But it was God down there, not dinosaurs, and I was connected to everyone else because we all had that same bright ocean at the bottom of our minds.

But it didn't make me feel any better. Instead I got crazier. My nerves began to shriek. I was no match for Carmen or anyone else. I had this weird idea she was amusing herself by poking me to see where I hurt and if she could make it hurt worse. I wanted to go live in a tree in Golden Gate Park or in a driftwood hut on a wild beach in Big Sur, somewhere where there weren't any people and I could sit in the wild mustard and look out to the crystalline sea until I felt better.

Solveig started seeing a shrink at the Student Health Center. I knew she was brave and adventurous and tough, but her life was tipping off track too. She'd ricocheted from a tentative marriage to a boardinghouse where she washed dishes for room and board, and from there to a sort of war zone on Judah Street. We'd only known her a few months, yet we were her only support system. She couldn't call home because she had no money for long distance phone calls, nor did her parents.

By now she was president of the San Francisco chapter of the Student Peace Union. She could speak clearly to large groups of students without rambling on forever like our more doctrinaire members. But the speeches were coming from the brainy part of her. Deeper down, she was starting to crumble. I just didn't know it yet.

XVII

We threw a party. Everyone came, the peaceniks and beatniks and San Francisco State artsy crowd and girls of every persuasion. Ronny Romola brought his Gibson guitar and Fender amp and fingerpicked electric folk melodies in one of the upstairs bedrooms, unfurnished except for a five-dollar mattress, a Modigliani print and a broken copy of *Growing Up Absurd*. He was on his way to becoming a junkie. In later years, I would see him scrounging on Haight Street. Once he asked if he could spend the night in my room because he had nowhere to go, and in the morning he stole my checkbook while I was out getting muffins. That was junkies, you had to expect that. But I was still mad he had stolen from me, and mad his talent had dissipated while he was nodding in grim Fillmore Street hotel rooms.

Downstairs, proto-hippies were doing the Pony like Bony Maroni, they were chatting up longhaired brunettes in peasant skirts and Audrey Hepburn lookalikes in pixie cuts. They were gulping Val-Vin burgundy from waxy paper cups. Smart drinkers had brought their own quarts of Olympia beer, and six-packs of Green Death, also known as Green Barf or Rainier Ale. A covey on the back porch was rolling that rarity, a joint. I was sitting on my own mattress in my own room, surrounded by my own fans of soulful children, singing how I was going to end my days in The House of the Rising Sun.

Local teens invaded the party about midnight. They shouted "Get the beatniks!" The beatniks turned out to be less pacifistic than the teens expected. I watched as Peter Weissinger, who had belonged to a teenaged Jewish gang in Queens before he moved west, dropped from the third floor landing onto the shoulders of an 18-year-old, laughing like this was the best part of the night so far.

I didn't know how to fight. I hadn't even been allowed to take P.E. in high school because of my heart murmur, which wasn't good and was slowly getting worse. I went upstairs to Tess's room and huddled beside her mattress. She was crying. I touched her brown hair. She was a good if slightly wild girl from Marin County, and she didn't know what she was getting into when she moved into the house on Judah Street. She wanted to go home. I comforted her and comforted myself by comforting her.

I couldn't find Carmen. I hadn't seen her in an hour. She had been in the main room, doing a kind of very cool, ultra-slow bop with Peter. She used to disappear that way, it wasn't unusual, but not at a party. She liked parties. Maybe she'd gone to the store for pretzels. I walked down the long hall, looking in each room at smokers and talkers and dancers in the dark. Somebody was reading Ferlinghetti's new broadside aloud. It was two in the morning. The party was winding down.

The door to Don's room was shut. An unpleasant suspicion whispered in my mind, and I knocked.

"Carmen, are you in there?"

What a fool.

Her voice came back softly, "Don't come in, Christopher. I'm not alone."

I kept walking down the hall, back to my room at the far end. There was no one there, nothing left of the evening but stale smoke and paper cups with dead butts disintegrating in the dregs of Val-Vin. I looked out the window at the clear starry night, and the weed-filled backyard with its grown-over goldfish pond and its clothesline with no clothes.

I looked out the window and then I pushed my fist through it.

Now I'd done it. There was blood all over the windowsill. I'd ripped a piece of skin off the heel of my hand and blood was gushing out. I left a trail of red drops down the hall as I went to find Solveig. She was still in the living room with her old lover Joe and her new lover Carl, peaceful together, all three. She bound my wound with a dish towel. I hunkered down on the madras-covered mattress with them in silence.

In the gray morning, one more time, I packed my clothes and books, and woke Solveig to say goodbye. She looked at me with sleepy eyes and sat up on the mattress and said, "Go well Christopher." I knew she meant it, and I was glad to hear it.

I caught the N car at the corner and rode it downtown to the Greyhound station and I got on the bus and rode home to San Mateo and walked down Railroad Avenue past auto shops and job printers and Southern Pacific railroad tracks stretching off to L.A. in the blue sky morning, and a freight rumbled by and I thought I saw Jack Kerouac in the caboose waving his railroad cap at me and calling, "Go well, man."

I cut across the salt flats with its puddles filled with skittering brine shrimp to my parents' modern plate glass house with my mother's abstract expressionist paintings on the mahogany paneling and my father's clack-clack rattling typewriter in his office and my brother's dusty dead bedroom with boxes on his unused bed. No one was home but Koko, the Siamese cat, who waved his tail and rolled over to have his stomach scratched.

XVIII

Mom said I looked terrible and took me to the doctor. He said I had mononucleosis, that I needed to rest and be quiet for a month. I read *A High Wind in Jamaica* and listened to Beethoven's Fifth on the hi-fi, but it made me weep, so I listened to lyrical Bizet but he sucker-punched me into tears too, so I listened to Top 40 in my room but it made me puke.

The month passed. Plum blossoms appeared on the tree in the garden, fluttering in the February blue. At least no one was home to see me weep like a fool. I wanted my brother, killed four years ago in a car crash, so bad I wanted to die too, except I didn't really. I had to go on and try to never imagine Carmen's sweet breath on my face again, because she didn't love me and would never come back no more.

Tess came to see me, Carmen's ex-roommate Belladonna wrote me letters. One night everybody from the house on Judah Street except Carmen and Solveig drove down. They sat in the living room while my parents were nice to them. Nothing about my friends ever fazed them.

To ease my suburban suffering, and I guess because he felt guilty about sleeping with Carmen, Don gave me his Mexican guitar, which is beside me now, scratched and weathered as the hand that writes these words. Anyway, I could play it and he couldn't.

Solveig wasn't there because she was somewhere in America, hitchhiking home.

XIX

After I left, Solveig got sadder, moodier. It wasn't me leaving, although we did sort of hold each other up. Unlike Shelly back in Florida, she didn't revel in sleeping with Joe one night and Carl the next. In fact, it was making her crazy. Her shrink suggested she follow her heart or some crap like that, but she couldn't. She didn't like her heart. There was no provision in its rulebook for having sex with two guys at the same time without loving either one. The only answer that would make her an acceptable human being was to love both of them. But which one did she love most? How could she tell when her stupid heart kept implying they were just hanging out together?

On the morning after the party, Solveig swept up the broken glass in the hallway, washed the dishes, emptied the ashtrays, made coffee, climbed upstairs to her room, shut the door, and lay on her mattress watching the watery light undulate across her ceiling. She wasn't anything her friends thought she was. She wasn't a speech maker, she wasn't a president, she wasn't a chairwoman, she had no ambition, she didn't care about school, she didn't love Joe or Carl, she wanted to go home and see her mother and her sister and her brothers, if they still remembered her.

Of course, she had seen them just last month, but her mother had been distant, there hadn't been a chance to touch. She had heard nothing from her family since then. It seemed unlikely she'd ever touch her mother again, ever be close to her like when she was little. She wanted, she needed, she needed, oh God she didn't need anything anymore, except to die.

Solveig turned on the open flame gas heater that was built into the wall, but she didn't light it. She put on her coat and her wool socks and lay down on her mattress and watched the ceiling and listened to the gas hiss.

An hour later, the heretofore unmentioned Danny Levandowski hiked up to the top flat to see if there was anything to eat in the upstairs kitchen. He smelled the gas leaking from cracks of Solveig's closed and locked door. I was in San Mateo listening to Beethoven, yet I think I heard him say *Shit* under his breath. He broke the lock in the door and shut off the gas and opened both windows, and took Solveig in his arms and carried her down the dusty hall into Tess's room and opened those windows too onto Judah Street to hear the N car rumbling by and children playing hopscotch and listening for the return of Don LeClaire, off somewhere on his motorcycle with Carmen on the back as seagulls wheeled and soared higher and higher in the February sky.

He knew she was alive. He could watch her breathing. Danny wasn't all that selfless of a guy and he had to get to his journalism class, but he couldn't just put her down and go about his business as if Solveig was taking a nap. So he sat beside the bed and waited quietly.

When Solveig opened her eyes at last and looked at the world through a sick headache, she saw Danny Levandowski, star reporter for the student newspaper of all people, smiling at her encouragingly. Danny hadn't said six words to her in his life before, but he'd pulled Tess's paisley comforter over her and sat beside her with his hand on her shoulder for companionship, so she would know in her sleep that she wasn't alone.

Solveig spent a couple of days drinking instant coffee and walking in Golden Gate Park, like we used to do together. She had registered for spring semester but she wasn't going to class. The compulsion to go home grew in her.

Carl told her he was going back to Iowa. He had no money left so he was going to hitch, take the northern route because it was faster. Solveig decided to go with him as far as Iowa City, then hitch the rest of the way by herself. She sent a postcard home to let them know she was coming. Two days later, they descended the front steps of the house on Judah Street for the last time, caught the Haight bus to Laguna Street, climbed the hill to the Oak Street on-ramp, and stuck out their thumbs.

XX

A young guy and a girl hitching together could get rides fairly easily in those days, and in a few minutes they caught their first lift, across the bay to Berkeley. Half an hour later they got their second ride, to Sacramento. Beyond Sacramento, traffic thinned. A young man on a ski holiday took them as far as Truckee. By eight o'clock that night they had their thumbs out just beyond a gas station in Lovelock, Nevada. Once they started, they had to keep going, 24 hours a day, till they reached Iowa City. It was too cold to sleep in the sagebrush, even if they had wanted to.

Hitchhiking at night wasn't that much fun. Long drives through the darkened West gave drivers ideas, especially after Carl dozed off in the backseat. About midnight, a middle-aged family man suggested she help pass the time by sucking him off while he drove. Solveig froze him with a look, then stared out the side window into the icy night until Carl woke up. She was disgusted, she was angry, and she was scared. When he stopped for gas, they grabbed their stuff and disappeared into the sagebrush until the "family man" had driven away.

A girl had to get used to it, though, because it happened nearly every time Carl took a nap. Outside of Wendover, a driver asked Solveig if she was "making it" with Carl. She told him they'd had a love affair but it was over, they were just hitching together.

"I'll pay you five dollars to let me watch you fuck," he said. They dived at the next stop. It seemed like half the drivers who picked them up wanted sex with Solveig.

As dawn broke, Solveig stood in the desert somewhere on the edge of Nevada in her little blue Keds, beside one of the two guys she didn't love any more, if she ever had, with her thumb stuck out, praying the next driver wouldn't murder them and leave their bones in a ravine for vultures to pick when summer came.

In Salt Lake City, they asked a wino where they might find a free meal and a place to sleep. He took them to the Joe Hill House, founded the year before by a Catholic pacifist/anarchist named Ammon Hennacy. He made it into a beacon in the desert for hoboes, drunks, and anybody else who needed a place to sleep and was willing to sleep on the floor. Anyone could stay as long as they didn't bring in a bottle, or start a fight, or piss on the floor. He didn't get that many student couples, so he offered Carl and Solveig his only private room, the Cooler, a closet under the stairs where drunks slept it off and sobered up. They rested and chopped carrots, and they slept.

Solveig dreamed that Neal Cassady and Jack Kerouac gave her a lift in their hot rod Lincoln, highballing nonstop all the way to Hyattsville, Maryland. In her dream, Jack told her mother still loved her.

She really wasn't feeling well, so they rested the next day, trading stories and hitchhiking tips with hoboes and other lost travelers. Someone gave her a scrap of paper with a phone number scrawled on it. He said, "If you get stuck in Wyoming, call this number."

They were heading that way, so she put the scrap in her purse.

XXI

As they climbed into the mountains beyond Salt Lake they hit snow again, and it got heavier as they neared Wyoming. They walked a few yards past a well-lit truck stop and put out their thumbs in hopes a trucker coming out would pick them up. While one waited and hitched, the other would warm up in the coffee shop.

At the pumps, Solveig said, "Please, please, are you going our way?" The drivers usually told her they weren't allowed to pick up hitchhikers. But eventually they got a lift. Slowly, slowly, in the snow, they reached U.S. 30 and crossed Wyoming. By the time they caught a ride into Cheyenne, Solveig had been standing in the snow for 12 hours in her little blue Keds. Her feet were frozen, her socks were wet, her teeth were chattering. And she didn't feel well.

So when they were dropped off at the Flying J Travel Plaza, they decided to call the number on the scrap of paper.

A woman answered the phone. They explained they were hitchhiking from California, and were freezing. She asked where they were and said, "Well, I have to pick up my son after school. Then I'll come and pick you up."

Her name was Sandra Harry, still in her late 20s, and part of the Catholic Worker movement like Ammon Hennacy at the Joe Hill House. Long afterward, Solveig told me, "They didn't know us from Adam; we had no references or letters of introduction. We called out of the blue. And then there she was, making room for us in their station wagon and showing us each our own bedroom with clean sheets and warm blankets and quiet. They had a troop of little children, all polite and sweet." They were homeschooling their children, which Solveig had never heard of before.

They sat in their living room playing with the children while Sandra made beef stew. They ate with the family, then she handed them bathrobes, told them to give her their clothes so she could wash them, to take a bath, then go to sleep. Solveig slept for 24 hours.

She had felt tired for days, even before they started out. She wondered if she was coming down with mononucleosis too. She hoped a good long sleep would cure her, but when she awoke, she was still tired, and now coughing. She thought she must have caught a cold from standing in the snow.

When they came down to breakfast the next morning, Sandra's husband was home. She served them bacon and eggs and toast and coffee, more if they wanted it. Carl *did* want more, and wolfed it down, but Solveig sipped her coffee and poked at her yolk. They talked. Carl said he thought he'd go back to college; Solveig told them she needed to be with her family for a while.

After breakfast Mr. Harry drove Carl and Solveig to the Greyhound station, bought them tickets and gave each 15 dollars for food on the way. He said, "You guys just go home."

Solveig said, "Well, let me have your address, so I can pay you back when I have the money," and Mr. Harry said, "Just pay it forward. Pay it forward." She never forgot.

They said their good-byes in Omaha, where Carl changed for Iowa City and Solveig transferred to the bus for Chicago and points east. They agreed to meet again in San Francisco in the spring. Solveig never saw him again.

XXII

Solveig slept her way through the snow-covered East, her head resting against the hair-oil-smeared window. Her head ached, and the road vibration didn't help. At stops she bought coffee, nibbled a doughnut, went to the rest-room, climbed back on board, and dozed again.

The miles finally wound down to the Washington Greyhound depot. Waiting for her father to get off work, she watched students in line for the bus to New York City, talking excitedly among themselves. Solveig only wanted to go home, climb into bed and stay there for a very long time, except it wasn't home any more.

She told her father she was pretty sure she had mononucleosis, but it didn't take him long to convince himself she was pregnant. That must be why she came home. That's what her health problem was. He took her to a doctor who understood problems like this. They spoke German to each other, he asked Solveig some questions, gave her an internal exam, and listened to her lungs.

She dressed, her father came into the examination room, and the doctor said, "Mr. Rimkeit, Solveig's not pregnant. She has walking pneumonia."

Later, Solveig told me, "And my father was so happy! It was the most loving he'd ever been to me. He was so scared I was pregnant! He was happy I had walking pneumonia!"

She was ordered to stay in bed for a month, and not get up except to go to the bathroom. She had to drink a glass of port every night to thicken her blood.

Her mother made her a bed on the couch in the dining room, there was nowhere else, and Solveig thankfully climbed into it. She went to sleep. When she awoke, she found her mother had placed a lamp behind her so she could read, and an end table beside her where she could keep her books and her Kleenex box, and she put the kitchen radio on it, so Solveig could listen to music. Then she quit her job so she could cook three meals a day for her dearest wild daughter. She went to the library downtown and returned with bags of books, whatever her daughter wanted, as many as the library allowed. Solveig worked her way through Norman Mailer and Durrell's *Alexandria Quartet*, Sartre's *Roads to Freedom* trilogy, and *Journey to the End of Night*. That's what she did. And then she was cured. And her alienation from her mother was cured too.

XXIII

Ah, Solveig, my old friend. Hard to believe you're as old and worn as I am old and worn. I see you still in my mind's eye with sunburnt wheat hair and pointy black-rimmed glasses slipping down your button nose. Still 19, gentle smile still playing over your lovely but not beautiful face. But beautiful, unforgettable in my heart always.

I remember when you returned to San Francisco after adventures up and down the east coast, you worried because your father's drinking was getting worse. You rented an apartment on Page Street in the ghetto and brought your 13-year-old cracking-voice brother to live with you so he wouldn't have to witness his father's downfall.

Later, you convinced your mother to come to San Francisco too and start over. You found a bleak, desperate but really cheap flat for her on Octavia Street under the Skyway, but she was afraid to go out, so you found her another apartment on Cabrillo Street in the quiet Richmond District, a block from Golden Gate Park. And there she lived for the rest of her life, as far as I know, because we began to drift apart. You married a guy and had babies and didn't have time to hang out any more. I never saw you, yet I loved you and could never forget you.

I saw you again one last morning in 1968, at the White Front drug store on 16th Street when I crawled in to buy aspirin, and you were in the diaper aisle in your poplin coat and young mother dress with no makeup, with your toddler daughter on your hip, slipped into another life while I was sleeping on the floor of a scattered apartment on Potrero Street, not my own, with boxes and dirty clothes strewn in the corners and the flotsam of somebody else's life invading my dreams.

We spoke politely to each other when I wanted to hug you to my heart and tell you how much I missed you, but you hardly knew me anymore and turned into other aisles to look for something that was never going to be in my aisle. Why didn't you remember?

I could not forget.

Leslie In The Crystalline Night

One night in December 1961, Leslie Hipshman and I were driving across the City at the Rainbow's End in my liver-colored Studebaker Lark. We weren't on a date, of course. Dates were uncool. It was just an ordinary Wednesday night in San Francisco and, for some reason lost in the mist, we were hanging together.

The night was cold and crisp – not crisp like eastern autumn nights when the leaves are falling, but crisp in clarity, the light exact, deep-focus, like it gets in San Francisco after a December rain and a windy afternoon. There was nothing left in the sky but clear sea air flowing over the downtown stockbrokers' offices, the Fillmore conk salons, and the desolate streetcar tracks of the Sunset District.

We weren't supposed to be together. Leslie was going with Don LeClaire, the leader of our peacenik brotherhood. Against my will, I was ending my painful love affair with, Carmen O'Shaughnessy. But neither of them were in the car. There was just Leslie and me cruising through the clear eternal night listening to somebody singing how he didn't like his mother-in-law and wondering what to do with ourselves. I knew what I wanted to do, of course. I wanted to park somewhere and hold Leslie tight. Leslie waves beat against me like radio signals. They came in clear as the air: "I'm young, I'm beautiful, my skin is like satin, and my hair is shiny black. I'm very, very delicious. And I like you too."

But you had to let these things take their course. Forcing yourself on someone was uncool and could lead to an unfortunate outcome. Besides, I didn't have designs on Leslie. We were just together, that's all. She couldn't help owning a powerful radio transmitter any more than I could help having a receiver that worked really well.

Leslie and I had never spent time alone with each other. Once we'd walked to the corner store together to buy Bugler cigarette tobacco. So we did what self-respecting young freaks did in the winter of 1961 when they weren't on a date – we headed for the wasted remains of North Beach. The era of the beatniks was over and the era of the hippies hadn't begun, yet we knew we were as happening as the beats had been. We just hadn't had a chance to show it yet. We were drawn like moths to the flame. But the flame had burned out.

Upper Grant Avenue, scene of epic cultural battles when Lawrence Ferlinghetti and City Lights Books stood trial for publishing a dirty poem called *Howl*, where Officer Bigarini had arrested beatnik chicks for wearing sandals in public, where poets like Bob Kaufman and Gregory Corso and of course Allen Ginsberg had broken free from writing airy martini-driven university puzzles like what professors required me to study in English 101 and instead shouted visions of backyard greentree cemetery dawns on street corners or riding the Muni or standing in the smoke filled Coffee Gallery declaiming while Jack Kerouac ran to the deli for more dago red. Upper Grant Avenue in its quiet desolation was our link to the mighty heroes of old, whom we would never admit we sought to emulate. We were just going to get something to eat and look for our friend George The Beast.

George was the biggest beatnik we knew. Of course, since I was 19 and Leslie was 17, we didn't know too many. I was pretending to go to college at San Francisco State and Leslie was still at Lowell High School, but George – George was living the full-bore life. With his army fatigue jacket and single gold earring, his hypothetical parrot on his shoulder, and his magic to make everybody laugh with joy at anything, George was the dog who trotted freely in the streets. Maybe he wasn't up there with Ginsberg and Corso yet, but hey, those guys were in their 30s already and George hadn't hit 20. Meanwhile, he slept where he could and cultivated acquaintance with the rotters, pimps, poets, and crystal merchants who congregated in the Hot Dog Palace after midnight.

We found a place to park on Commercial Street jammed between a vegetable truck and a red zone. Out the door lay the land of tong wars and Fu Man Chu, of sweatshop lights glimmering behind curtains in the night, of dripping roast ducks and squirming fish in the butcher shop windows – Chinatown, the penultimate scene for San Francisco romance, and I was walking through it with a beautiful unknown continent beside me. Before us lay the tiled stairs that led to the coolest of Chinatown's cheapest restaurants, Huey Gooey Looey, where the beat elite meet to eat.

In the winter of 1961 and for many years thereafter, Huey Gooey Louie's was the restaurant of choice. Maybe it still is. Nowhere were the waiters as surly and the chances of meeting someone you knew as likely as at Huey Dewey Louie.

We slid into a red vinyl booth, ordered fried wontons with sweet and sour sauce, and leaned back, maybe wondering who that person was sitting across the table. I'd moved into the peaceniks' flat on Judah Street a month before to live at the nerve center of our scene, and Leslie had come with the territory. To see Leslie and her high school pals Relay and Teresa ensconced on Don's mattress playing guitar, listening to Joan Baez or Ray Charles, was as normal as looking to see if anyone had done the dishes yet.

One other thing I should mention about Leslie. She happened to have "IT," as they used to say about Twenties movie star Clara Bow. She wasn't exceptionally beautiful. She didn't attempt to be sexy or provocative. But something about her made young guys like me turn their heads to see her walk by. Perfume emanated from her that you couldn't smell, but it smelled good anyway.

Now here we were at Huey Louie Gooey's, leaning back, waiting for the won-tons, waiting for the world to end, waiting for our lives to begin, and talking about the inconsequentialities of the day. Some friends in the peace movement were going to drive across the country over Christmas break. They were going to march in front of the White House waving placards to make a little mark against death from the skies. We knew it was hopeless. But we couldn't just sit there.

Leslie couldn't go but I thought I would. Then we moved on to Joanie Baez, whom we loved, and Miles Davis and John Coltrane. Her father collected jazz records; she'd grown up listening to the greats. She even knew about the Dixieland guys from long ago. That was cool. I liked a girl who stood up for something, even if it was only Dixieland jazz.

I don't think I had noticed before how intelligent she was, how full of brimming life, eager to experience the full range of human possibility. Restless, reckless, a little crazy, I just took it for granted – we were all like that. We didn't talk about it. And of course I noticed her shining black hair cut in a Dutch boy bob. Of course I noticed how she filled her bulky-knit blue sweater against the booth's red vinyl. Her easy laugh. Even her slightly crooked teeth were cute. Why couldn't I be in love with her instead of the braided, insane wild child who teased and tortured me, driving me insane too, but my craziness was to want her more and more? Leslie was reckless too, but in a different way – I felt easy and comfortable with her.

Like every other restaurant in Chinatown in 1961, Huey specialized in Cantonese delicacies. Besides fried wontons they offered pork fried rice, cashew chicken, seaweed soup with little pink shrimps swimming through kelp beds in the bowl. I'm sure they had more exotic food over on the Chinese side of the menu, but for Leslie and me, fried wontons were still pretty exotic. After the meal, I splurged and treated her to Hooey Dewey Gooey's signature culinary delight: shivering, quivering, glistening almond pudding with a nut in the center and a canned mandarin orange slice and a fortune cookie on the side. We took bites from the gelatinous substance in our bowls as Leslie told me about her life as a hip high school kid. It wasn't a lot different from my own life as a high school hippie in San Mateo, the suburb where I'd learned to hate suburbs.

On weekend nights, Leslie told me she'd get home by curfew, make a show of going to bed early, brush her teeth, flush the toilet, yawn, then make a body shape from pillows under the blankets and sneak out to meet her beat-wannabe friends. No one had a car, so they walked through the city, down to Market Street, or over Russian Hill to North Beach. There they patrolled its back allies to see if any big beat parties were still going on. Maybe one day they'd catch Jack Kerouac running out to the late night deli on Broadway for even more dago red. But they never saw him. Maybe they saw his shadow once.

We were all under his shadow.

Next we headed for Lawrence Ferlinghetti's great information station for the underground world, City Lights Books. By now we were comfortable with each other and enjoying the night. Finding George The Beast became a handy reason for wandering around the best neighborhood in the best city on the best coast.

Shig was at the counter as usual, leafing doubtfully through some baggy poet's self-published tome. We checked for George upstairs and down, and poked around the poetry section. I leafed through the new issue of *Sing Out!* to see if it had that plastic record in the back so you could hear how the songs sounded. Two months before, high on peyote, I had listened to Joanie Baez sing "The Great Silkie" on one of those vinyl pull-outs, listened to her over and over until it was inscribed in my consciousness. I wanted another one of those little records if I could find it.

George wasn't anywhere around, so we browsed until we were bored, then crossed Broadway to check the Hot Dog Palace.

The Hog Dog Palace, fabled hangout for junkies, beat wannabes, angelheaded hipsters, posers and hosers, also known as the Amp Palace or the Meth Palace for the ampoules of methamphetamine a speed freak could easily score there – maybe it was grim, cold, fluorescent, unsanitary, but it was really really cheap. From its fly-specked windows you could see everything and everybody making it down Columbus Avenue or even Upper Grant if you snuck up the back stairs and peered through the glass door. The Hot Dog Palace stood on the site of Pandora's Box, which in its day had been a genuine pseudo-beatnik sandwich shop where they served Zen Soup to sip while wearing Zen slippers and pretending to read *Beat Zen, Square Zen, and Zen*. It was kicks, man, kicks! And they kept getting harder to find.

George wasn't there either, but I saw Pat Lofthouse scribbling cartoons in his sketchbook with a Rapidograph like he always did. And I saw Gypsy Boots, a street hustler who made his living doing things with other men I didn't want to imagine. Gypsy was shoveling quarters into the jukebox like they were slugs. Maybe they were. I guess he was in the mood for Jimmy Reed singing "Bright Lights, Big City" because we heard it three times in the 10 minutes we strolled from table to table.

Looking for George was getting boring. We decided to walk on up Grant Avenue. There were no more hangouts up that way unless you were over 21. I wondered if Bria was in the Anxious Asp. She was the first lesbian kid I knew I knew, and she could pass for 21. She was usually drinking in the gay Asp or somewhere nearby.

The question in my mind was – should I take Leslie's hand? Were we at that point? I wanted to. I liked her. But...well...I didn't want to look uncool in her eyes. Cool people didn't hold hands while they walked along. That was it. Unfair, but true. The rules were the rules.

The moon rose, silvery and full, its mysterious light rolling past us as we hiked toward Greenwich Street. At the corner we passed the laundromat that had been Pierre DeLattre's Bread and Wine Mission, where poetry and bongos and Jesus and hipsters – made for each other, really – had touched and kissed and sadly parted. The moonlight glimmered on the laundromat's red neon sign 15 CENTS WASH. 10 CENTS DRY. We kept going. Pierre didn't live there anymore.

Such a beautiful night. Why not walk on up the hill, all the way to Coit Tower, the floodlit phallus that pierces the skyline for 50 miles on a night like this. None of the city's Manhattan style high-rises had been built yet and the City still looked Renaissance, magical, from up there. Let's go look again.

We turned right up Greenwich. The street was lined with pastel-colored narrow flats climbing in the moonlight like in some Italian hill town, Verona maybe, where Mercutio was stabbed by the Jets while Romeo screamed. Maybe Mardou Fox had lived in one of those flats when Kerouac mourned for her in *The Subterraneans*. Years later I learned Jack moved his story from Greenwich Village to North Beach because his publisher said it would sell better. *Oh, protect yourself, angel of no harm, you who've never and could never harm and crack another innocent in its shell and thin veiled pain*...the inventor of spontaneous bop prosody had shifted locales at the advice of his marketing director. He'd done it so smoothly I never even wondered.

At the top of Greenwich a narrow staircase led into the trees. We climbed on through the spooky city park darkness. Did I touch her? Our spirits were beginning to touch, just a little. Spidery tendrils of...what? Friendship? Understanding? Whatever it was, we were wrapped in it, and it was nice. The tendril webs were going to prove strong enough to link us across the continent as we tossed through squalling marriages, and stayed strong enough to urge me to keep her letters for nearly 50 years. I'm not sure those spider web tendrils have a name, but they wrapped round us like ectoplasm. They weren't named romantic love, and surely not just friendship – you don't want to hold a friend tight in the moonlight. Whatever it was it felt good. I had enough problems with passion at the moment. Who needed more?

We eventually emerged into a clearing beneath the great illuminated tower, its white stone turned golden by the floodlights. A half dozen couples like us, plus several melancholy gents perhaps looking for kindred spirits, wandered hither and thither in the moonlight. Leslie and I sat on the damp grass and looked out over the City at the Rainbow's End sparkling crystalline in the December night.

The ramparts of the Shell Building lit in blue-green shimmers, the parapets of the Russ Building flooded with gold shimmers, they beaconed over the Renaissance city like Doge's towers, papal towers, Aztec towers, Inca towers – over the great city that sprang from the sand dunes on the far Pacific shore. And we were sprung too.

You probably didn't know native-born San Francisco kids can be just as manic about the town as any fresh arrival from Dubuque. On a crystal December night from the top of Telegraph Hill we could feel somehow we'd been accidentally born in the perfect place.

Leslie said, "City's sure beautiful tonight."

I said, "Yeah…"

I didn't mention the other nights I'd sat here, usually with my high school pals, occasionally with a girl. Leslie didn't go into her past either. The light descended upon us and into us. I had no plans beyond loving this night, this city, and this sweet girl beside me – all in pretty much the same way. Generalized and without any particular future.

We thought we knew what we wanted. Leslie wanted to be free from sitting in rows waiting for the bell to ring, free from her mother's plans for some wrong future, free to go where she wanted, to find out who she was, who she could be.

I was already free to be blown wherever the wind blew me, if not free from the chains of the Skyway. What I wanted was someone to love forever with the freedom of complete equals. Someone who would want to go see where Mercutio got stabbed that starlit night, an adventurer comrade who would also be beautiful and very very hot.

It was eight years before I got her. And she came with kids and responsibilities.

We sat there a long time, talking quietly and then not talking at all. Maybe this moment was what we really wanted.

Eventually, though, the damp seeped its way through our jeans. It was a weeknight, anyway. Leslie needed to be home by 10:30.

When we hit Greenwich Street again, Les decided to run. She wasn't really in that much of a hurry. Screw curfew. But the hill was so steep and we were so full of moonlight that when she took off I peeled out after her, catching up and grabbing her hand like we were kids or young lovers in a New Wave movie, running and laughing and trying to go yet faster but stay in step. Cats looked up from their garbage cans in surprise. The old man walking his poodle turned to see more of this beautiful girl and the freak with the Buddy Holly glasses trying to beat each other to Grant Avenue. We careened around the corner onto Grant laughing breathless and didn't stop until we passed the Coffee Gallery where we hugged each other as drunks shouted encouragement out the door and tossed quarters.

We kept going now just walking past the Fox and Hound where we could hear Jorma Kaukonen playing Delta blues inside on his slide guitar. Back past the Hot Dog Palace – through the window we saw George the Beast standing at the counter jawing with Fast Walker Johnson. But the night was coming to an end.

Aw, there'd be other nights. Hundreds and thousands of other nights in the city of our hearts where the fog never lifts and the moonlight never ends and the wind blows always bright and clean. George wasn't going anywhere and we'd be young forever.

We drove across the City again over Russian Hill down past Van Ness and out through the Fillmore to Leslie's mother's flat on Baker Street. Miles was blowing "Freddie the Freeloader" on the radio and the night was sacred.

I double-parked in front of Mom's place so Leslie could jump out but she didn't jump out. I didn't want her to jump out. We were illuminated, bright, and I took her in my arms and we kissed. We took a long time. We could have kissed forever as far as I was concerned. But then it was over and she did jump out and in through the door and she did look back at me before diving through, *Hi Mom!* I drove back to Judah Street levitated a foot off the front seat.

Did we fall in love and live happily ever after?

Did we save up together to go find where Mercutio was stabbed?

Or did the wild child Carmen O'Shaughnessy finally break up with me forever and then did I finally completely disintegrate and catch mononucleosis and go home to recuperate in the suburbs and there did I meet a girl at a party in Burlingame and didn't we split for Pacific Grove three days later and didn't she get pregnant that summer and didn't we marry and live together in love and misery and didn't Leslie run off to New York with Wayne Gellerman when she turned 18 and didn't she get pregnant too and didn't she give up her son for adoption but find him again years later as I found Leslie's letters again in a dusty box and wrote to her and didn't we meet each other again one time more when we were old?

Would it have been better if we had found George The Beast and gone off to his hotel room and smoked pot all night? Or if Leslie had caught a cold and stayed home?

What does this scanty story mean, anyway? For that matter, what is the meaning of life? I have no idea, of course, but it might have something to do with little tendrils that sometimes creep out in the moonlight. Sometimes they grow into strong cables like the ones between my wife and me. Tested and true, no matter what. And sometimes they never grow beyond a tentative little spider web. But either way – they're the best things God gave us poor humans.

How I Almost Met Neal Cassady

In the spring of 1962 I was hanging out in San Francisco's North Beach with my new girlfriend Linda Lovely and the raffish denizens of the Hot Dog Palace. We spare-changed tourists and dropped by the parish hall at St. Peter and Paul's Church opposite Washington Square for free hard-boiled egg sandwiches (it actually *was* a hard-boiled egg, still in the shell, between two hunks of French bread, wrapped in newspaper like fish and chips).

My pal George The Beast had snagged a job as night clerk at the Hotel Dante, next door to topless pioneer Carol Doda's club The Condor. The Dante was not like hotels of today with chocolates on the pillow and turndown service. The Dante was a Sam Spade dusty dim light hallway hotel where real men in fedoras and revolvers in shoulder holsters thought existential thoughts while staring at the bare lamp bulb screwed above their single bed. Outside flowed Columbus Avenue, with its million stories of hard luck dames and baby-faced gunsels, and Ambrose Bierce shooting it out with Bret Harte as foghorns groaned and cats cried in the night.

One afternoon, George says to us, "Hey, you want to see Neal Cassady's room?"

"Well....duh!" I sez to George, using an anachronism since no one had yet realized "duh" could be a catch phrase.

Cassady was just out of San Quentin. He had been busted for possession of marijuana and been sacked away in Q since 1958. Back in those days, a guy could go to prison for years if a cop stuck his hand in your coat pocket and found a joint.

Even in 1962 Neal Cassady was a legend – *the* Dean Moriarity of *On The Road*, and of course we wanted to be within the glamor circle of his greatness, a real legendary member of the real beat generation. He wasn't anything like me and Linda Lovely and George The Beast, not quite sure who we were, wanting to be real beatniks and looking like real beatniks, but actually 20 years old and acting a lot like kids who had memorized *Howl* and thought *Dharma Bums* was a treatise on right living.

This was about four in the afternoon, nothing was happening in the "lobby" of the Dante – a narrow foyer beyond the front door with stairs leading up and George behind the counter grinning like a bodhisattva with his gold earring gleaming. So George leads us up the stairs to the second floor and down the dark passage to an even darker doorway on the right-hand side.

"There it is – that's Neal Cassady's room."

I could actually feel the beat emanations exuding through the door. Was he behind it writing long mad letters to his famous pals? Was he out looking for another joint to stick in his pocket? I'll never know. We waited around for lightning to strike, and when it didn't we looked at each other and shuffled and finally went back down to the lobby and laughed and joked until George got his dinner break. Then we walked down to Huey Looey Gooey's and ordered three bowls of seaweed soup.

The Baby Beat Photographer

In the summer of 1962 I took a course in photography at San Francisco State from Jack Welpott, a modernist photographer of renown. He said my stuff was sentimental.

His words cut like a knife. Me? Sentimental? No way! I was bad as they come. Look at this guy! That's me, the very summer of my mortal wound. I knew the streets. I knew grifters. And I knew what sentimental meant: cheap emotion manufactured to give the viewer a cheap thrill. "Oh, look at the cute little kitten and the big dog is carrying it so gently. Isn't that sweet?" Pictures like that were sentimental and I had nothing to do with sentimentality.

Linda Lovely, as she was.

Could I help it if every time I looked through my viewfinder there was a sad-eyed, vulnerable waif looking lost and forlorn?

Gypsy Girl, as she was.

I wasn't taking pictures for a cheap thrill. I was taking pictures of my friends, the girl variety to be exact. That's how they looked, so beautiful my heart ached and I wanted to give them to the world forever, which I now do.

Sheila, as she was.

I wasn't sentimental like that Walter Keane, the laughing stock of the baby beat world. He and his wife ran an art gallery on Broadway above a topless bar, and sold his sad-eyed little waifs with huge eyes to tipsy tourists who stood in line to see.

Bleaah! Sickening! Me and Linda Lovely and Russ Garibaldi and Gypsy Girl and all my way out friends laughed cynically as we passed the Keane-bound crowds on our way to an important meeting standing outside the Jazz Workshop to listen to John Coltrane because they wouldn't let us through the door. Tourists! My pictures were nothing like those soppy paintings. They were... uh... well... my girls were older for one thing.

Oh why, ye gods? I go forth to capture the true nature of the human heart, and, in particular the true heart of my various girlfriends and what do I get? Your stuff is sentimental! By a big time modernist like Jack Welpott who must know. I was crushed.

Even when I went forth to shoot approved modernist subjects like severe nudes with no heads, weathered barns in the gold rush country, or Edward Weston style barnacled rocks looming out of Pacific tide pools, I got ruined castles, I got broken dreams, I got enchanted princesses in long gowns and wimples sleepwalking through haunted landscapes.

Botheration! I give up! I'm a stoopid romantic! I'd better not tell anybody.

San Francisco's Palace of Fine Arts, as it was.

Of course what I didn't know is that the modernist fever was breaking. Within a couple years young barbarians would be ransacking junk stores looking for Maxfield Parrish prints, and new poster art would be created by artists who cut their teeth flame-painting '49 Mercs. And not a minute too soon for me. Eat your heart out, Jack Welpott.

Into The Hard Day

San Francisco

1962-64

Baby Beats Seek Truth Too

In my distress I cry to the Lord,
that he may answer me:
"Deliver me, O Lord,
from lying lips..."
Psalm 120

I wanted God in my life. I longed for Him/Her/It. But, near as I could tell, the Biblical God was not really God. For instance, I read Psalm 18 about God riding down to Earth on his thundercloud with smoke coming out of his nostrils. Did Christians really believe he created the entire universe and then went riding around shooting lightning out of a thundercloud? How could they take this stuff seriously?

That's how I felt, I'm just being honest, okay? At 19, this was an issue about truth for me. And it's still a valid, if sophomoric, question. In a world that was full of lies and deception coming at me from every corner like whizzing arrows – which is how I felt and every truth-seeker has to feel – why should I believe one religion's version of the truth is the right one just because they insisted that it is? Coca-Cola is the real thing too, according to Coca-Cola.

Kerouac's novel *The Dharma Bums* presented me with another option – seeking God through direct experience. As I saw it, the book was about three guys searching for God, and God is Truth. That's what Dharma means. In one episode, Kerouac and poet Gary Snyder (under novelistic pseudonyms) go on a mountain climbing quest in the Sierras. I could see that climbing the mountain was really about two things -- first, going on an adventure with great wild friends, and second, about getting higher into the pure truth and out of the smog of the world's lies and hypocrisy. Direct experience, enlightenment. Real proof because it happened to you!

And there was another scene where Jack (I think this is actually in *The Subterraneans*) sits in a library in the Santa Clara Valley day after day surrounded by spring cherry orchards and reading the Diamond Sutra. I didn't know what that was, but it seemed to be some kind of teaching where you didn't have to believe all these stories about God riding around on his thundercloud. He was – Something Else. Unknowable. Ineffable. Something beyond understanding. Both personal and impersonal. Encompassing everything. Wow! I felt that must be the way God is. Really Big!

Were there any Christians around to show me what Jesus was all about? I didn't hear anybody knockin'. In fact, in all those long years from high school to 1968, when I encountered my first Jesus Freak, there was not one person who defended or even spoke to me of the Christian faith with a fair understanding in a way I could comprehend. If I didn't ask – well, who was available to ask?

Okay, that's a fair question, let's see. At San Francisco State there was the Campus Crusade for Christ. From time to time, they would set up a table outside the Student Commons, handing out tracts and stuff. At the next table over there was another group called the Young Americans for Freedom. They espoused every right-wing position available in the early Sixties, from supporting Madame Nhu's repressive but anticommunist dictatorship in Viet Nam to trying to elect arch-conservative Barry Goldwater president. Members of both organizations wore the same short-sleeved white shirts and skinny black ties. They wore the same crew cuts, and carried the same kind of book bags. I wasn't sure, but I figured maybe they were both part of the same organization. And, to me, they both looked like The Enemy.

I don't remember ever being "witnessed to" by a Campus Crusade guy, but if I had been, you know what I would have said? "The only thing I want to be saved from is having to spend eternity with guys like you! How dare you try to 'save me,' whatever that means? You know nothing of the pain I suffer. You haven't earned the right."

No preaching, no witnessing, no handing out of tracts would have had the slightest effect on me. If they pointed out some eternal truth from the Bible, I could counter with an eternal truth from *Bambi*. They were both just books!

You know who I might have listened to? A Christian girl I was in love with. If she spoke earnestly and I could see that through her life that there was truth in what she believed, then I would have given Jesus a fair shot.

Second best would be if I heard about him from another freak. Someone whom I trusted who spoke to me about his own experience. Not a preacher dressed up in hippie clothes, but one of my close friends.

I wish I had known about a secret church of dirty beatniks who were at war against the Great Society of lies and malice for all. In other words, people who were really living out Jesus' teachings. I would have gone there in a New York minute.

Now that I think about it, I still want to go to that church.

Rodney

Rodney Albin about 1974 (photo: Maya Cain)

I guess of all the friends I had back then, in the halcyon days of my hippie youth, Rodney Albin is the guy I miss the most. When he ditched this planet in 1984 – stomach cancer got him when he was still a young man – I felt like I was losing my brother all over again.

133

As with so many of my folknik hippie commie friends of the early Sixties, I met Rodney kind of like this...

Late one morning in, I suppose, the fall of 1962, I exited San Francisco State's HLL building, where the boring part of my initiation into high Western culture took place, and ambled across the lawn towards the Commons to get coffee and see what was up. Despite its medieval-sounding name, sheep were not pastured in the Commons, nor did peasants, other than us, trudge there every morning to work their land. The Commons was a roaring cafeteria in the center of campus, where everything of consequence that happened to me in those years began or ended – either inside its doors at the second table on the left or on the lawn directly in front of it. There it is in the center of the picture below, as it looked in 1960. Who could guess a nondescript building like that would become a cauldron of Sixties counterculture?

San Francisco State campus in 1960, Commons in the background.
(photo: San Francisco History Center, SF Public Library)

On this particular morning, I happened to notice a new guy sitting cross-legged on the lawn, surrounded by the regulars and passing around a dulcimer he had just built. He was a tall, prematurely balding kind of folknik, just transferred in from a community college on the Peninsula. It was his dulcimer that was extraordinary.

I forgot about the coffee and squeezed into the circle. That dulcimer was pretty cool, all right. With soft flowing curves like Jayne Mansfield, strummed with a seagull feather, you could tune it to any interesting modal scale you might be in the mood for, brush its strings with that quill, and there I was, mournful and lost in the holler, sounding like I'd been born in Viper, Kentucky, instead of San Francisco.

It sounded like magic, and this guy had created the damn thing from a piece of spruce he'd found in somebody's garage.

I got to know Rodney after a while and discovered he and his brother Peter were still living with their parents in an upper-middle-class neighborhood in the Belmont hills. I also learned that Rodney wasn't the new guy – I was. He was already well known in folk circles up and down the Peninsula and across the Bay in Berkeley. He'd masterminded the folk music festival at the College of San Mateo where Jerry Garcia made his debut to an unappreciative audience of frat rats. Rodney and George The Beast had opened the Boar's Head the preceding summer, a coffeehouse in the loft above the bookstore in San Carlos where George worked. Garcia and the other Palo Alto folkniks regularly showed up there to jam into the weekend nights.

I started dropping in to see Rodney when I was down that way. On my first visit, he showed me the six-string balalaika he'd built out of orange crate wood. It was his first crude try at building an instrument, but I could play it and it stayed in tune and it was made from a box he found on the sidewalk outside Mrs. O'Toole's grocery store. Here it is in the photo on the next page (that's his brother Peter holding the guitar.)

Peter and Rodney about 1960. Rod holds his handmade balalaika.
Peter with his first guitar, a Stella. (Photo: Peter Albin)

He was way beyond that now, of course. He'd finished a viola da gamba, and now he was building a harpsichord on his bedroom floor. Its parts spread hither and thither across the carpet; tools, a reel to reel tape recorder and an unmade bed filled the rest. He used the tape machine to record performances at the Boar's Head. Some of these tapes still exist and are passed from hand to hand in Deadhead circles. On them you can hear 1962 versions of Jerry Garcia and Ron McKernan (Pigpen) of the Grateful Dead, David Nelson (New Riders of the Purple Sage), Rodney's brother Peter (Big Brother and the Holding Company), and other less talented performers who went on to become teachers and bureaucrats and welders – but still played pretty good.

Rodney opened a new world to me. Before Rod, folk music meant Joan Baez manning the barricades while Pete Seeger fired his musket at the Pentagon. It was about peace marches, sit-ins and drinking dago red at parties while somebody plunked out "Twelve Gates to the City, Hallelujah" on a nylon-string guitar.

These friends of Rodney's were not exactly serious, but still dedicated to what they were doing in a way I hadn't seen before. They listened to Charlie Poole and the North

Carolina Ramblers on scratchy 78s. Was Charlie from Greenwich Village or Boston? I wasn't sure. They sang about chickens loose in the barnyard squawk and they tried to make their music sound as much like those scratchy 78s as they could. It wasn't that easy. They worked at it. I couldn't imagine why they were trying but, hey, I liked Rodney so I listened and tried to understand.

I just didn't see how "Boil Them Cabbage Down" would save the world from nuclear destruction.

Rodney's younger brother Peter was already an accomplished musician, although still in high school. He could wail on "Boil Them Cabbage Down" but then roll right into John Lee Hooker and come out the other side playing Chuck Berry riffs. And deep inside, I still preferred rock and roll.

Rodney and Peter at the family home in Belmont, about 1962.
(Photo: Peter Albin)

Rodney was kind of unusual looking. He had a classic beanpole shape, gawky you might say, and sniffy too. Since none of us (at this point) had ever tried cocaine, he must have suffered from allergies. His thoughts were punctuated with snorts and sniffs. He could stay wrapped in his old overcoat on the hottest day of the year and be perfectly comfortable, and his stomach was already bothering him, he would have to dose it with slugs of half and half that he kept handy.

With a body like his, he was born to play comedy roles, and he worked it. The first time I saw him (as opposed to meeting him) was in a production of *Twelfth Night* put on by the College of San Mateo drama department. I'd gone to see an old friend of mind, Ricky Lazaro, play Malvolio. Ricky was an experienced actor and knew how to get laughs, but when Rodney as Sir Andrew Aguecheek entered stage right, Ricky just gave up. Rodney wandered in as if he wasn't sure where he was supposed to stand, then stood rubbing his nose, looking around as if he couldn't quite remember his lines either. The audience slowly began to titter and he built the moment into the play's biggest laugh. He worked that role successfully for the next 20 years.

A few days after Rodney passed his dulcimer around, I was sitting on the grass trying to impress some proto-hippie chicks by playing "I'm a winin' boy, don't deny my name" on my Mexican guitar. I was using a crappy two-fingered picking style I'd invented. My thumb kept the rhythm while my index finger picked out the melody, and the effect resembled a crab attacking some worms. If I hadn't been a soulful singer, the chicks would have walked. As it was, they were listening, but they weren't looking at me like, "Oh, can we go to bed with you right now?"

When it was Rodney's turn to do a song, he launched into "Freight train, freight train going so fast," singing it in his trademark thin nasal voice. I thought his singing could use some help, but, man, he had that Elizabeth Cotten–style finger-picking right down! His thumb was rocking between the bass strings and he syncopated the melody like the old girl herself! Actually, I'd never heard of Elizabeth Cotten, but whoever she was, I wanted to play like that too. But how could anybody make three fingers work together like that? Maybe I should stick to my authentically primitive crab style.

Rodney encouraged me. He showed me the moves over and over till I started to get them. I went back to my apartment and drove my old lady, Linda Lovely, mad singing the silly thing over and over with my thumb rocking and fingers trying to syncopate it right, "Please don't tell what train I'm on so they won't know where I've gone."

Linda was thinking, "When's that train leaving?"

Come Christmas, Linda, in a moment of madness, gave me a mandolin. She'd found it in a Third Street pawn shop and bought it for $20. I was thrilled. I loved messing around with instruments and could play a lot them, all by ear and without much skill. I asked Rodney if he knew how to play one and it turned out he did. He showed me how to hold a pick and how to play a simple tune. After I mastered that, he taught me a more complicated minstrel song called "Colored Aristocracy." After that, I didn't need any more lessons. I knew four chords and could pick two songs. I was ready to roll!

I didn't know it yet but I was about to take my place in the Albin Brothers' shape-shifting band, the Liberty Hill Aristocrats. One night, Rodney said they were going to play the Top of the Tangent in Palo Alto and they needed somebody to play rhythm on mandolin. I was a mandolin player! So next night, with some trepidation I got up on the club's little stage, playing with or in between Jerry Garcia and Peter Albin and David Nelson – real masters of their instruments. Rodney didn't care if I only knew four chords.

That was Rodney, he got people going, and he included them, even if it affected the professionalism of the music. He had his priority list, and friends were higher up than professionalism. You had to love a guy like that, and I did.

A Child of the Century

Today Nathan Zakheim is an art conservator in Los Angeles, world renowned and bald, but in 1963 Nathan was the most rambunctious leftie folksinger at San Francisco State, bold and brave, with mounds of curly black hair, cheeks of kibbutz health and a boasting black beard. Nathan dressed the part too – he looked like he'd just hitchhiked out of a 1930s CCC work camp and was about to grab a freight train across America to the big Wobbly meeting in Tacoma.

Not that it was an affectation, you understand. I dressed exactly the same way. So did everybody else on the scene in those days, except for Ale Ekstrom, who dressed like a 19th century tar and played sea shanties on his concertina.

At this late date, I don't have Nathan's set list, but I'm sure he sang about the galvanic labor struggles of 50, 60 years before. I'm sure he sang about Joe Hill, the Wobbly organizer who'd been shot down by a firing squad in 1914, but was still an inspirational figure from the mists of time to the rebels of 1963. He sang "You can't fool me, I'm stickin' to the union" and "Solidarity forever, the union makes us strong." And of course he blasted out the Russian folk anthem, "Meadowlands"

> *Meadowlands, Meadowlands,*
> *meadows green and fields in blossom,*
> *Merrily greet the plucky heroes,*
> *heroes of the Soviet Republic!*

Hey, I'm not talking politics. Who knew about politics? Mine began in rage because someone was about to drop an H-bomb on my head, and ended with hoisting Ban the Bomb

You Bastards! placards at semi-nonviolent demonstrations in the Civic Center Plaza. When I sang "Meadowlands," every verse was meant to be a Dada snowball thrown at the pillbox hat of uptight SQUARE America and its weird right-wing defenders – the Christian Anti-Communist Crusade, the John Birch Society, the Ku Klux Klan, and, of course, George Lincoln Rockwell and his American Nazi Party mates.

Nathan lived in the dust of a communal flat on Divisadero Street with an 18-year-old magician named Willie the Wizard, a would-be sorcerer who called himself Edmund Robere, and Rodney -- luthier, folkie, and brother of my heart forever, though he would laugh to hear it.

On a day in late February 1963, my girl Linda Lovely and I picked up Nathan and Rodney in my beaver-colored Studebaker Lark – we were heading for Rodney's big house party at his uncle's place on the Russian River. He'd invited everybody who was anybody on our scene to play music under the redwoods till we dropped. On the way, we delivered a few supplies to Nathan's father, who lived on a small farm outside Sebastopol. It was on our way.

Wild mustard flowers shouted to us from the apple orchard as we turned down the road to the farmhouse. Unshaven but smiling, Bernard Zakheim came to the car to greet us. In those days, Zakheim was a forgotten giant of Bay Area art. His unrepentant socialist politics had put him in trouble with the Art Establishment since the Thirties, when he'd painted one of the anti-capitalist murals in San Francisco's Coit Tower. It wasn't that radical, really, it simply showed a library patron reaching for a copy of *Das Kapital*. But the morning paper screeched that Stalinist propaganda was now being honored on government-sponsored walls. Zakheim refused to repaint the title to read something like *How to Win Friends and Influence People*. The newspaper stayed flustered, the Art Commission blustered, but Zakheim held his ground, and eventually the whole controversy blew over. The Coit Tower murals are still there today, silent reminders of the time when artists had the guts to speak out against an oppressive system.

Zakheim found it harder to get work as a muralist, and by 1963 not many remembered him. He didn't look too unhappy about it, though. He served us tea and sugar cookies. We smiled. I didn't know what to say. I guess I could have asked him how it felt to be a giant from the ancient times. It didn't matter anyway, he wanted to chat up my girl, the sylphlike Linda Lovely.

We drove on. Raindrops glistered out of the sky. We seemed to be driving through a Grant Wood painting or an unknown Zakheim mural. A chocolate brown car in purple light chugging along a two-lane highway with work booted children inside listening to rock and roll.

We turned right at Occidental, and followed the dripping valley into a redwood forest. The light dimmed. The air smelled musty and poignant. I switched on the headlights as Rodney pointed out directions to the dank and mildewed vacation house.

There it was, under the trees. Friendly lights glowed through the mist. Someone was tuning a banjo. Someone else had got the woodstove going and someone yet else had set four gallon jugs of Old Chateau Burgundy on the trestle table. Dave and Nancy Parker were at work on the spaghetti sauce and French bread and green salad. Everything was happening in the kitchen, the only warm room.

More cars began parking along the shoulder, what there was of it – Palo Alto bluegrass players, College of San Mateo banjo frailers, San Francisco State dulcimer girls and Berkeley versions of the Greenbriar Boys.

People found floor space to spread their sleeping bags, the kettle of spaghetti was finished off, and guys started tuning their instruments. I'd never seen so many shiny D-28 Martin dreadnoughts – they were the bluegrass flatpicker's dream instrument, and Gibson Hummingbirds with necks that almost played themselves, and vintage Stellas, the country blues player's choice, and even an occasional plywood Harmony trying to fit in and look like it belonged. Kind of like me.

Okay, I was jealous. I was sporting a Mexican nylon-stringed guitar with a cracked soundboard and tuning machines that wouldn't stay in tune. It might have been good for sitting by the lake and singing love songs to the moon. Here, it was shy and wanted to hide.

A smiley Palo Alto kid with short hair and baggy clothes kicked off the night with some mighty good Scruggs-style banjo picking while singing a bluegrass tune called "The Hit Parade of Love."

Now, understand. I liked the blues, I loved John Coltrane, *La Boheme* knocked me out, I even liked the girl groups like the Shirelles who were popular on the radio. But I had to draw the line somewhere and this sounded like a good place to start. This cornball "Hit Parade of Love" stuff, this nudge-nudge-wink-wink "Happy landings to you, Amelia Earhart" (which came up next), these "Don't send my boy to prison for that would drive me mad" absurdities were driving me right against my principles. Next they'd be wanting me to pull a few choruses of "How Much Is That Doggie in the Window?" and join in on high harmony.

But, on the other hand, was I missing something?

For me, folk music had always been something I sang at parties. I had fun entertaining people, they enjoyed it, The End. I'd done the same thing in high school, riffing off of Richie Valens and Buddy Holly tunes. But now I was in a roomful of serious players, guys who copied hillbilly music from scratchy 78s note for note. And they clearly loved it.

We were in the same room, but we were in different musical realities. I didn't like broken-glass harmony. I didn't like thin voices singing reedy through their noses. I couldn't understand why these perfectly interesting, creative and entertaining people wanted to play such cornball music. I was polite, I was interested, but I wasn't buying it.

I wished good old Pigpen McKernan was here with his blues harp. Maybe he'd show up later. We knew all the same

Jimmy Reed songs. We'd both spent our high school years listening to KWBR, the R&B station that beamed across San Francisco Bay from the ghettos of Oakland to Republican San Mateo, and where I was reminded after every song I could buy a complete furniture room group for $99 at the Furniture Discount Warehouse – and, where I first heard Bobbie Blue Bland shout,

> *"She used to call me Bobby, Little Boy Blue,*
> *B-O-B-B-Y, BAH BEE!!"*

The hairs on the back on my neck stood up and shivered. Then James Brown and the Famous Flames came on singing

"Please please pleeze darlin' PLEEZE don't go!!!"

Lying in my suburban middle-class bedroom at midnight, the music stabbed me in my own teenaged terrified heart – heartbreak and rage, but over what? I didn't know over what.

I liked these people and wanted to be friends, but I couldn't grasp their idea of good harmony. I'd grown up listening to what people today call doo-wop. Back then there was no name for it, it was the way black guys sang when they improvised in church halls or street corners. Driving around bleak San Mateo after school, with its class divisions and crickity postwar subdivision stucco emptiness, the sorrowful major and minor sevenths soaring into the seagull sky – that music made sense to me, beautiful and complete. It helped me keep going.

Well, it was a great party anyway. The rain poured down but we stayed warm around the woodstove and played unbroken music and I did end up joining in on the high harmonies. Linda disappeared after a while. Chicks usually did that, unless they were players themselves. I couldn't understand it.

Too bad. She missed the one Palo Alto guy at the party who was more than semi-good. His name was Jerry Garcia. Slender, goateed, with a cowboy hat and a five-string banjo, I could tell he was seriously good although I knew nothing about banjo music and wanted to know less. Then he put his banjo down, picked up his guitar and did the same, then he put the guitar down and picked up his fiddle and did the same thing all over again. He was so far out of my league, I just gave up and grinned.

The next morning Linda and I struggled out of our zipped-together sleeping bags and went to find warmth and coffee. There by the stove I heard two Palo Alto folkies feeling sorry for Jerry. Their conversation went something like this:

"Poor Jerry, when we get out of college we'll get good jobs and move on to the serious world of grownups while Jerry – what does he have to look forward to? He'll be shuffling from Bakersfield to Fresno and back, playing in country and western bars the rest of his life. What a dead end. Poor guy, somebody should talk sense to him."

That afternoon, longhaired Linda and our baby-to-be and Dave and Nancy, we drove aimlessly down the rain soaked February roads of the Russian River country. We bought French bread and cheese and salami and sat on a storm-washed log at Jenner Beach watching the gray-green breakers roll in, roll out. We drove the coast highway to Fort Ross where Russians had piled sea otter pelts and waited for the great sailing ships from far Alaska. We followed a one-lane farm road into the sheep-dotted hills in the mist and then more redwood forest.

Somewhere out there, I can't remember exactly where but we weren't stoned, we came across a deserted building, little more than a cottage. Its door hung open. We stopped to see. Mushrooms grew on the threshold. I pushed the door open, scraping off mushrooms, moss. Mice and spiders watched us from corners, without curiosity so far as I knew. Dim light seeped through the gray bolted sky. Shelves lay toppled across the moss green floor. Hundreds of musty books lay where they fell long ago. Most were mush by now.

It must have once upon a time been a country library. Sheep ranchers' children must have come on Saturdays to borrow *Caddie Woodlawn.* Then, who knows why, the librarian walked off into the woods and left the library to molder. Sheep nudged in from the rain and left their calling cards. I found a still-legible novel under a fallen-over half-rotten bookcase. It was called *Confessions of a Child of the Century.* But which century? I took it home to San Francisco, dried it out and tried to read it. The Greenbriar Boys were singing "Life is like a mountain railway with an engineer so brave, we must make this run successful from the cradle to the grave." But the pages were stuck together and I couldn't make the story out.

Can Scotch Broom Flowers Get You High?

Even though I was born and raised on the California coast, I knew nothing about shooting the curl, waxing my board, hodads, wiping out, any of that stuff.

I was from Fog City, man. I never drank Coors Beer from tan cans. When I went to the beach, I went to San Francisco's North Beach, "where there isn't any wadder and Big Daddy ain't your fadder," as the old song says.

What, you never heard that song? It was very big on Upper Grant Avenue in 1962. Late-arriving beatniks in peacoats and sandals sang it in unison as they strode through the swirling fog to the Ant Palace for another night watching out the window as Officer Bigarini rousted less fortunate artists and poets.

What did we know from Gidget and Moondoggy? We went to the movies to see the divine Marie Dubois get shot down by that comical crook in the snow at the end of *Shoot the Piano Player*.

What? You never heard of that movie? It was very big with ratty student scruff as they huddled in their peacoats against the damp of the night ocean air on Judah Street on the way to the Surf Theater to see it for the 81st time.

Sometimes we'd get tired of watching Marie Dubois get shot down so we'd go see Jean-Paul Belmondo get shot in the street like a dog at the end of *Breathless* because of that traitorous turncoat American itchy-bitchy blonde Jean Seberg, who looked a little like Gidget.

Is this clear? Fine, then let's talk about eternal verities for a while, like Mimi Fariña.

What, you never heard of Mimi Fariña? She was very big in the cold plastered kitchens of incandescent Haight-Ashbury flats in 1966. *Reflections in a Crystal Wind* was the LP she put out with her beat poet husband who got smashed on his motorcycle just as his career was taking off. I can hear it now ringing in my ears along with Donovan's *Sunshine Superman* and Country Joe and the Fish's first album. That was about it for music in our hippie student commune on Frederick Street the fall of 1966 thanks to my insufferable roommates the Gunderson twins. They couldn't ever think of more than one thing at a time and the thing they thought of was to play *Reflections in a Crystal Wind* again. Interrupted my studies of the *Goldberg Variations*, but what could I do? I know. Smoke more dope.

Only 19, Mimi's legend was already huge in the Underground. I won't bother to mention that she was Joan Baez's little sister. That's so demeaning to the great lady who went on to found Bread and Roses, the organization that brings performers to prisons and hospitals and orphanages. She ran it till she died of cancer a few years ago.

Those Baez girls – unbelievable how they affected all of us. They proved there were some people out there who were like us except more beautiful and nobler and could sing better. And knew Bob Dylan.

I saw Mimi perform at a party at Big Sur Hot Springs in 1964. David Crosby was there too (what, you've never heard of David Crosby?) and he was just one more very good Big Sur folksinger. But Mimi! There was a hushed air of expectation in the smoke-dark rooms of the rusty redwood resort. Mimi was coming! Her legend, her mystique was already rife. Joanie's little sister, she had to buck up under her big sister's Queen of the Folksingers aura.

Mimi's actual singing is a blank to me, I'm afraid. I see her in a pool of saintly angelic light, the scruffy crowd of Vikings and timber beasts and vegetarian moon meditators all hushed and dragging on their Camels as her pure voice sang "Cripple Creek."

That night we drove to the back of a nearby canyon and hiked up to Crazy Mary's creekside cabin in the redwoods. That was the summer a rumor swept through the Underground that smoking Scotch broom flowers could get you high. Relay Tornfoot and I were in Big Sur to investigate this hypothesis. We asked somebody what Scotch broom looked like, then we picked its little yellow flowers all afternoon, stuffed them in a corncob pipe and inhaled deeply. We passed the pipe around to other experimenters. We went outside the cabin to gaze up through the redwoods at the starry post-Mimi Fariña night sky. They glittered no more brightly than before.

"Do you feel anything, man?"

"Maybe. I think I might be feeling something. Give me some more of that."

One more thing. The night before, camping in a field back from the coast highway, we saw Lawrence Ferlinghetti and his girlfriend walking through the field. He was wearing a wide-brimmed hat and speaking to her of ineffable, wonderful things that we could never know.

What? You've never heard of Lawrence Ferlinghetti?

Song for Relay Tornfoot

Relay, if you are still on this planet
And bones not moldering with Wyatt Earp's in Colma graveyard.
If you are still scuffling the streets of the Fillmore in toebrokethough tennis shoes and not
chained in a state institution somewhere.
If your first-born child knows your face
and thinks of you at all
or even if she
don't,
here is still a song for you, my sad-eyed comrade.

First saw you barefoot,
cross legged, eighteen,
Lowell High School drop-out,
top school in the city drop-out,
Don LeClaire's new drop-out sidekick.
You marched for peace together,
LA to San Francisco in the long ago 1962
arrested, went to jail
it was all the same to you
Before your intelligence was sucked like juice from an orange.

There's you and Don now
lounging cool on ratty mattress,
bare except for Carmen's holey Mexican blanket,
dirty red, dirty yellow,
LeClaire laughing like he had a flea.

Heavy rim glasses slipping down his nose,
black mustache crinkling.
You were heroes to us,
Come home to Ithaca Street.
You were beautiful,
surrounded by hippie girls,
Relay, they loved you and made much of you.

There's Teresa Sweet,
red haired
freckled
seventeen
already married to Red Mike, doctrinaire commie.
he wanted to move to Yugoslavia,
Teresa to North Beach.
Or Berkeley.
Big Sur would be far enough.
And Leslie Orchid too so
cozy,
touchy,
feely,
lounging between you both,
hot for you, Relay, but loving Teresa.
Leslie was Don's girl,
hair silken black
skin satin
seventeen too.
Lived with her rich mother
on fogwet Pacific Heights.

You remember Leslie, don't you?
Sweeter than Sweet, brought her Bob Dylan album.
"His voice so scratchy but nice," she says,
Nobody heard of him before.

Relay, you sprawling
smiling

silent
what were you thinking that morning?

The four of you so young
and cool
and free as I look back on you through time,
your long
sunny,
moony
youth ahead of you.
All of you.
No pain no suicide, no madness I see
as you pass the jug from hand to hand,
the thin slivered joint,
the terpen hydrate,
Romalar,
amyl nitrate,
peyote buttons,
Marlboros.

Relay, you had a blue sweater
April sky color.
I could see you coming through the fog,
sitting home on Sacramento Street,
reading comic books,
cutting out pictures for collages,
wondering what the fuck,
with baby daughter napping in the bedroom.
We'd get high and
laugh and
listen to Lightin' Hopkins, then you'd leave again,
stoned and alone.

Relay, blue sweater tornshoe,
I came by to see you in your
one room pad on
Fillmore Street.

Madras bedspread,
greasy window,
but you were gone to score.
Your lady,
blonde beat girl
alone and large with child,
she stuck by you and kept your child inside
and you out to cop.
Only white girl on the block,
She took care of you both in
lowdown Fillmore cribs you lived in,
none for long.

Relay, you got heavier into drugs,
heroin, I suppose though
I don't know and then
I didn't see you any more except
once flitting down a back street, sad specter.

I was dressed in brown. You thought
I was driving truck for UPS,
congratulated me on getting such a well-paid gig.

We shook hands in the gutter,
at the corner,
Haight and Masonic, and you
disappeared into traffic.
Disappeared into traffic like
you'd never been there at all.

The Summer of the Hard Day's Night

As the summer of 1964 began, I still listened to rock and roll in the car but only because I'd listened to rock and roll in the car since I was 14. I'd heard the Beatles singing "Love Me Do" and "I Want To Hold Your Hand" but they made no impression. In June, Ringo Starr changed planes at the San Francisco airport and 800 shrieking fans shut the place down. I glanced at the story in the Chron, yawned and turned the page. I watched a piece about them on the six o'clock news and agreed they looked kind of hip with their long hair and wise mouths, but so what?

So I didn't know what to make of it when my photographer friend Bill Laird, an ultimate bohemian with sad transparent face, green corduroy sports coat frayed at pocket and straggly black beard told me he had seen *A Hard Day's Night* with his old lady and they had stayed to see it again and I had to see it too.

A teenager movie? Incredulous but not wanting to miss anything, Linda Lovely and I and Bill and his girl Muttsie got stoned and braved the crowds of teenagers at the Saturday matinee at the Metro. It was true what they said about the nonstop screaming that made it impossible to hear the soundtrack, but, I had to agree these guys were...uh...incredibly cool.

From the moment early in the film when they make their escape down a train corridor, hide in a mail car and John whips out his harmonica and starts "Love Me Do," Ringo is playing a trap set that somehow materializes among the mail bags, and London birds with John Lennon caps pop into gleeful existence, my heart and mind were won over. We knew they HAD to be potheads like us. We stayed to watch it three times.

The next day I went to Woolworth's on Market Street and bought the soundtrack. The Beatles blew into our lives and took over. The sound track never stopped. We listened to Top 40 with fresh ears. Even Peter and Gordon sounded pretty cool.

And that is how the old bohemian world came to its end in a matter of weeks in San Francisco in the summer of 1964, how the Beatles, the Rolling Stones and the Kinks took their place at the top of the LP stack, and a new era began, the era of the dance concerts and the rise of Jefferson Airplane, Big Brother and the Holding Company and the Grateful Dead – the great acid rock bands of San Francisco.

Sally Go Round The Roses

"The roses they won't hurt you...the roses they won't hurt you."

What were the Jaynettes singing about anyway? We had no idea, but it sounded important. Their 45 single was mysterious and weird and it was the hottest song on our scene up at the Langley Porter Psychiatric Day Care Center for Mind-Blown Freaks and Hysterical Proto-Hippies, which included me, Peter B. and Loretta W. We'd play that simple but not simple Top 40 hit, "Sally Go Round The Roses," over and over again, feeling out its secret meaning. It sounded like heartbreak and fear, but also like it was Mashed Potato Time. Then we'd put on Buffy Sainte-Marie and listen to her sing *"I'll reel and I'll fall and I'll rise on codine."* That was clear enough, we'd all done the same thing, more or less.

It was September 1964. I was temporarily in the bug-house after finding myself hanging by my thumbs out the bay window of our flat on Golden Gate Avenue, Hayes Valley, San Francisco, laughing like a fool.

It hadn't been a bad summer, really. Like I said before, even Peter and Gordon sounded cool. They were English. They had Beatle cuts.

"I don't care what they say, I won't stay in a world without love..."

Another song I was mad about, now forgotten, was Shirley Ellis's "Let's Get Down To the Real Nitty-Gritty."

"Some people know about it, some don't."

I guess *I* know about it, I thought as I hung out the window by my fingernail fragments. Enough of grim reality, enough of suffering. I'm shutting my mind off as of this moment. Here I go. Into the great eternal Now. Yes!

Having made my decision, I climbed back in through the bay window and waited expectantly for the Great Now to appear. What would it feel like to live with no past to remember, no future to groan over? No future left nor past? The Zen moment. Ah! An apple! Shall I touch its blistery skin?

So, next day I'm sitting cross-legged in Washington Square, talking to an older friend about my newfound decision to eliminate the negative, discard the past and refute the future. I'd forgotten he was studying to be a psychiatrist and that he had a part-time job at the newspaper where my father worked.

Next thing I knew it was Thorazine and "Sally, don't you go downtown." I was in the bughouse, with Peter B., later one of the founding Diggers (look 'em up), also having a momentary lapse of judgment, and Loretta W., the first lesbian I ever knew except I would have called her a dyke.

In September 1964, as far as I knew, the sexes were divided into straights, dykes, and fags. I was blind to the implications of those words. Peter B., on the other hand, saw them clearly and called me out on it so many times in his off-center, New York hipster way, always talking a little over me, a little beyond me, that I was surrounded and started to understand what he was talking about.

He had a lofty intelligence, but in 1964, he still preferred to stand on the sidelines, smiling ironically.

Anyway, Loretta and Peter and I were pals. After a hard day at the bughouse, we would adjourn to a Fillmore District bar for a shot of red-eye. I studied Peter's words, his facial expressions and his half-smiles. I wanted some of that east coast hipster cool, too.

Loretta, on the other hand, taught me about attempting suicide and how it might get you into Langley Porter. She was older than me – at least 30 – and had had a sad awakening in the shower with her Marin County lover. She never explained exactly what happened, and even though I was dead curious, the right moment to ask her never arrived.

"Saddest thing in the whole wide world – see your baby with another girl."

Loretta looked like George Harrison. Pixie cut, rail thin, blue jeans, scuffed tennies and a man's dress shirt with the tails hanging out. She was screwy as a loon but much funnier than a loon. We played badminton together and went roller skating together and laughed at each other's wisecracks in group therapy. We drove to L.A. over Christmas and slept at her other ex-lover's house in Coldwater Canyon, not together of course. There was nobody home so we drank her friend's scotch and looked out over the L.A. lights and played the brand new *Beatles '65* nonstop and had a fine time, just the two of us.

"Oh dear what can I do, baby's in black and I'm feeling blue, tell me oh what can I do?"

Peter B. never laughed. He was New York sardonic. But he saw deeper than me or Loretta. We were sad clowns but he saw the truth about the corruption of the world, or at least he had thought about it, while Loretta and I were more thinking about the Beatles and the ouch inside our respective hearts. When we felt anything at all, which was hard to do when you're loaded on Thorazine.

I gave up on the Thorazine after a couple of weeks. I wasn't schitzy, I was just having a medium-sized adjustment problem. Okay, even if I really was crazy, I'd rather suffer than feel nothing. Or maybe Langley Porter with its cute psychiatric nurses who knew how to do the Mashed Potato, and my psychiatrist who listened and smiled and nodded and said nothing until I wanted to scream at her, maybe they worked their therapeutic magic on me. Maybe I just needed to be in a safe place for a while.

I checked out and moved to the Haight-Ashbury, not ready to face my future, but definitely ready to get into my present. Peter, you moved there too, but we got into different scenes. Loretta, I never saw you no more; I heard you went back to L.A. But both of you, if you ever read this, thanks for being my pals when I needed some pals.

History of San Francisco's Underground 1961-65

All the famous hippies emerged from blue denim
workshirts like butterflies in May 1965.
Except of course for one who
saw the old sun setting in
morning glory's
light,
golden, gleaming, intriguing, beyond
the freight car door.
He stepped from that box car
into it bright,
and wished all the rest of us
merry good
night.

R.I.P.
Gary Marxon
1943-1963

The Ghosts in the Corner

George The Beast Is Gone

George The Beast Howell, king of the Baby Beatniks, roarer of Upper Grant Avenue, companion of my North Beach youth – died at a quarter to six one morning not long ago in an intensive care unit at the West Anaheim Medical Center. He wasn't that old, but his body was shot. He'd had a lot of adventures, did a lot of drugs, smoked a lot of Camels.

167

Here's the only photo I have of George. I took it in Russ and Sue Garibaldi's living room on Sacramento Street in July 1962. It's not that great a portrait, and I never printed it, but I kept the test strip, and here it is, still good 50 years later, preserved by that good Community Darkroom photo fix, flies, cigarette ashes and all. But I feel like part of me is fading.

George wasn't a luminary of the Haight-Ashbury. By the time that scene gelled, George was living in a Mexican village learning to weave. Eventually, weaving evolved into hunting down and restoring antique rugs. He made a lot of money doing it. He had his own shop in a fashionable San Francisco neighborhood. His profits, most of them, went up his nose or into his arm. He was a man of big hungers and little caution. He went bankrupt, fled to Hawaii to clean up.

I still want to write his story, but I only know bits and pieces he told me over the phone after we reconnected. I thought there was plenty of time. We'd get together and hang out and talk for days until I'd heard everything, then I'd get it on paper it for everyone's illumination. That was my plan.

George's character was bigger than his body and spilled into the streets around him. We spent foggy nights walking from Mike's Pool Hall to the Hot Dog Palace and back, looking for friends, finding them and standing on the corner together till Officer Bigarini walked by and told us to beat it. We were in love with the same girl. We laughed about it. We were both 19, then 20, then 21 and we wanted to be beatniks. It seemed like the only sensible career, and, in a way, still does.

George, how can I come see you now?

People I loved have been dying on me my whole life and it's a dirty trick. I still want to go see everybody, but where? I feel I've been left behind to walk the beach in my overcoat at the end of time, and write it all down for no one. So that's what I'm doing.

Chet Helms, Carmen O'Shaughnessy and Me

Let me begin by saying Chet Helms had his moment of glory – a long, extended moment – as one of San Francisco's two premier concert promoters. You might say he was proprietor and maitre d' of the San Francisco Sound. Along with Bill Graham, he made sure the Jefferson Airplane, the Grateful Dead, Quicksilver Messenger Service, Santana, Big Brother and the Holding Company and, of course, Janis Joplin got right to the front tables and smoked the best dope in America.

I knew Chet pretty well in the Haight-Ashbury days, and we stayed in touch for a long time after. Here's a story about the manner of man he was.

By now you know that at the age of 19, I fell in love with a beautiful and cruel 17-year-old named Carmen O'Shaughnessy. On our first date she danced naked in the rain. I thought stuff like that only happened in books. I'd never met someone up to her style before and I fell hard and passionately. Not to put too fine a point it, Carmen ripped my heart open and drove me mad. But she was worth it. What a girl.

OK, fast forward 28 years. I'm happily married, a salaryman with a big New York career, living in a heartwarming but drafty Victorian in an country-quaint New Jersey town, laughing at old Bob Hope movies on TV with my daughter, and generally having a pretty good time of it.

Then, suddenly, I come down with a high fever, a *very* high fever. The doctor slams me in the hospital and I begin to see fever visions. In the night, tossing on my sweat-drenched bed, I suddenly discover I am 19 years old again. I am standing under a street light in L.A.'s Silver Lake neighborhood, across the street from Carmen's house. There are lights on in her house but I am alone under the moon and I am howling like a coyote, long, agonizing pain-racked cries of grief for Carmen, my lost one. When I awoke, I was astonished to discover I had a gaping wound in my heart covered with the finest of skins. Not one drop of hurt had evaporated in all those 28 years, and I hadn't even noticed it.

When I got to feeling better, I wrote to Chet about my strange experience. He had been around in those days and knew the players. I never heard back from him, but about three weeks later, I did get a letter – from Carmen O'Shaughnessy.

She was a grown up too. Lived up in the Rockies somewhere. She had kids. Still played her flute in the moonlight sometimes. She was sorry she had hurt me so bad. She was ashamed of her 17-year-old self.

I was surprised to get her letter, but not all that surprised – I recognized her handwriting right away. And I was glad too, because somehow the letter brought closure I hadn't known I needed.

Carmen had been in San Francisco for the first time in years and she happened to run into Chet on Market Street and he happened to have my address in his pocket. So he told her about my letter and gave her my address.

That was Chet through and through. Always right where he needed to be. Always knowing what was going down in all the flats in the Haight. Just had his finger on it. And he still did.

I Pay A Visit To Chet Helms

When I was in San Francisco the other day, I dropped by to visit my old friend Chet Helms. I knew right where to find him because for the foreseeable future, Chet will be residing with the artists, musicians, bankers, captains of industry, and possibly Emperor Norton at a swank retirement getaway in the Richmond District known as the Columbarium of San Francisco.Except no one gets away.

I stopped at the reception desk to see if Chet was in. He was. The receptionist was new and couldn't tell me his apartment number, but the manager came out of her office when she heard Chet's name.

"Are you here to see Chet?" she asked, implying a certain familiarity. "You can go right up." She rattled off Chet's rather involved address on the third floor and I pawed for my notebook to jot it down. She had it memorized, so I figured Chet must be getting a lot of visitors.

As I walked up the stairs, I could hear workers pushing a scaffold across the marble floor below and shouting to each other, something about Carlos Santana. I thought, "Oh no, what new bad news haven't I heard?" But I checked when I got home and Carlos is doing fine. I guess they just liked Carlos Santana. I kept climbing.

Chet's keeping a low profile these days. All boxed in, you might say. Not so long and tall as the day I met him in the summer of 1962. Here the picture gets all misty and we dissolve through to a busy San Francisco street filled with fishtailed cars and buses spewing exhaust fumes...

The old Greyhound Bus Station on Seventh St. in its 1964 glory. (SAN FRANCISCO HISTORY CENTER, SF PUBLIC LIBRARY)

That day I was hanging out at a protest on the steps of the main post office at Seventh and Mission, tuning my Mexican guitar and entertaining the picket line with my faultless impersonation of Joan Baez singing "I'm a rake and a ramblin' boy."

I had nothing against the mail being delivered, you understand. The federal district court was located on an upper floor and the judge was hearing the case against the crew of the Everyman, a trimaran that had sailed into waters scheduled for atomic detonations. Ka-Boom and all the little fishies were to receive their first dose of strontium-90. It was the age of "atmospheric testing," and apparently someone still wasn't sure if H-bombs worked or not, because they kept testing them and testing them. I thought it was a bad idea.

The story of that protest deserves to be told in detail – it foreshadows all the demonstrations and sit-ins and eventually the mass student strikes that characterized my youth. But at the moment, I'm watching a skinny young guy with lanky hair and black-rimmed glasses come out of the Greyhound Bus Station across the street, see the demonstration, and jaywalk over to see what's up. And, well, look at that, he's sporting a peace button. As you've guessed, it was Chet, fresh off the bus from Austin, Texas. I had the fortune to meet him during his first hour in San Francisco, scene of so many destinies, including Chet's and my own.

I hate to admit it but in those days I only associated with people who passed the coolness test, and was quite ready to snub any impostor with a Texas accent, but I could not snub this cat. Chet's ingratiating smile, his little heh-heh laugh, his unfeigned interest in everyone – within an hour he'd made the acquaintance of most of San Francisco's peacenik community – I liked him immediately. And he was back the next day, don't know where he slept. He was standing right in front that night when the real Joanie Baez showed up and sang on the post office steps to encourage us. Maybe he tried to sign her for a gig at the Avalon, I get mixed up sometimes.

Funny – all those years ahead of him, full of friends and rock and roll and great parties and fame of a sort, but now they're over. Now Chet's residing in a vase, a big doorstop. Dust, our common fate. To quote the prince of Denmark,

> *Imperious Caesar, dead and turn'd to clay,*
> *Might stop a hole to keep the wind away.*

Oh dear, am I growing grave? At least Chet has his own apartment, not far from Harvey Milk's place. And he'll never have to leave San Francisco again.

Three Girls Barefoot; Last Day of 1969

On the last day of December
Nineteen hundred and sixty nine,
three hippie girls stood far on a hillside
to watch the old sun sink.
Storm wind rising
swept their beads, their long hair flew,
chopped through their velvets,
chilled their warm young breasts.
Across the hill they made their way
back to their hidden cabin.
From its window spilled a light,
yellow, frail.
Inside, the baby cried.
Three hippie girls hurried faster,
their paisleys brushed against
red poison oak.
At their door, the youngest lit a joint.
In the wind,
in the dark,
on the hillside,
two hippie girls' eyes turned red.
The third, inside, was already nursing her child.

Acknowledgements

Thanks, all of you, my first few friends, for revealing yourselves to my inner eye so clearly I could still see you young and beautiful. It's good to look back to those days of yesteryear, no matter what John Lee Hooker says.

The stories are all true; some are truer than others. I've written about the life we lived fifty years ago and I might have got some of it mixed up.

To protect privacy, I've changed some names, as well as a few identifying details.

I particularly wish to thank Peter Albin, Howie Harris, Greg Hoffman, Marilyn McGrew, Leo Sadorf, Leslie Van Gelder, Rochanah Weissinger, Eva Wilson and my wife Patricia for their ongoing support as I worked to get this right.

Uncredited photos are from author's collection. Poster 2005 Tribal Stomp celebration is uncredited. Every effort has been made to obtain permissions for copyrighted materials; if I missed something, I apologize and shall be pleased to make appropriate acknowledgments in future editions.

About the Author

When Christopher Newton was young, he hit all the pot parties, made love to the willowy woodsy-nymphsy chicks, played guitar in parks and coffee houses across America, refused to become a pop star and spurned every opportunity to make scads of money. He wasn't even sure what a scad was.

Yet today he lives happily ever after with his curly haired wife at the top of a hill in Spokane, Washington, where he is writing the novel that will explain everything to everybody and nothing to nobody.

Made in the USA
San Bernardino, CA
10 January 2014